Adventures in
Python®

Adventures in Python®

Craig Richardson

WILEY

This edition first published 2015

© 2015 Craig Richardson

Registered office

John Wiley & Sons Ltd, The Atrium, Southern Gate, Chichester, West Sussex, PO19 8SQ, United Kingdom

For details of our global editorial offices, for customer services and for information about how to apply for permission to reuse the copyright material in this book please see our website at www.wiley.com.

A catalogue record for this book is available from the British Library.

ISBN 978-1-118-95179-8 (paperback); ISBN 978-1-118-95184-2 (ePub); 978-1-118-95185-9 (ePDF)

Set in Chaparral Pro 10/12.5pt by SPi Global, India

Printed in the United States by Command Web

To the swans on the river Cam. May you never visit the Fellows of St John's College.

Publisher's Acknowledgments

Some of the people who helped bring this book to market include the following:

Editorial and Production
VP Consumer and Technology Publishing Director: Michelle Leete
Associate Director–Book Content Management: Martin Tribe
Associate Publisher: Jim Minatel
Series Creator: Carrie Anne Philbin
Executive Editor: Craig Smith
Project Editor: Kezia Endsley
Copy Editor: Kezia Endsley
Technical Editor: Alex Bradbury
Editorial Manager: Jodi Jensen
Senior Project Editor: Sara Shlaer
Editorial Assistant: Claire Johnson
Proofreader: Wordsmith Editorial

Marketing
Marketing Manager: Lorna Mein
Marketing Assistant: Polly Thomas

About the Author

CRAIG RICHARDSON is a freelance software developer and writer based in the UK. When Craig first started using computers in his early teens he had a typing speed of one word a minute and successfully broke several machines. Since then he's studied computer science and software development at school and university and has taught hundreds of people to program with Python. He also now knows how to fix the many computers he breaks.

Acknowledgments

This book would not have been possible without the support of my friends and family. Cambridge Make Space has been invaluable: the reliability of the old Internet connection really helped me finish the book. I'd also like to thank the book's editors and members of staff at Wiley for their hard work.

Contents

Adventure 7
Creative Ways to Use a Mouse with PyGame 161

Adventure 8
Using Images with PyGame 181

Adventure 9
Using Sounds and Music with PyGame 203

Introduction

ARE YOU AN intrepid adventurer? Do you love trying new things and learning new skills? Would you like to bring your own ideas to life with technology? If the answer is a resounding "Yes!" then this is the book for you. Your adventures with Python start here! During your adventures you'll learn a lot about programming with Python. You'll create some really fun programs along the way, including games and animations.

Before you take your first step, take some time with this introduction to understand what you'll be doing and answers some of the questions you might have.

What Is Programming?

First off, what is programming? Put simply, programming is giving the computer a set of instructions to do something you want. For example, when you play a computer game programs determine what the game will do when you press a button and what is displayed on the screen.

Just as programming is giving the computer a set of instructions, a **program** is a set of instructions that has been written by a programmer.

You write these instructions using a **programming language**. There are many different programming languages, which you can think of as similar to human languages like English or French. Each programming language has its own way of doing things but they all share the same fundamental concepts.

A **program** is a set of instructions that has been written by a programmer to instruct the computer to do something.

A **programming language** allows you to give instructions to a computer. With a programming language you can create programs that control what your computer does.

As a programmer, you have a lot of choice when choosing a programming language to use. So why choose Python? Well, Python is a good language to learn for beginners. It is designed so that it is relatively easy for humans to read. The layout and words it uses for its instructions make it easier to learn than other languages, such as Java or C++. Python is even used in the real world—in fact, it is one of the most popular programming languages used by professional programmers, who use it to do all sorts of things, from analysing scientific data to making games. You can see an example of some Python code in Figure I-1.

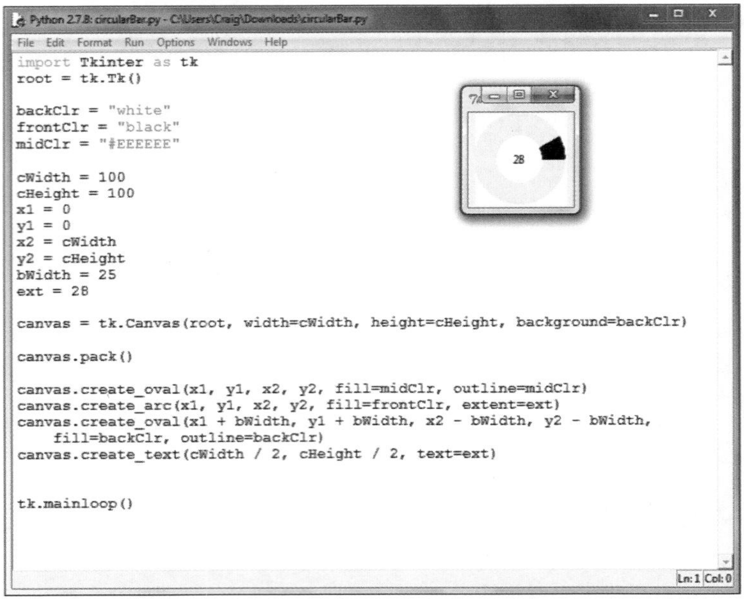

FIGURE I-1 The code of a program that generates a circular progress bar. You will learn how to create programs like this one in your adventures.

This introduction is intended to help you get set up with Python on your computer. It's here to make sure you start your journey on the right foot and have everything you need to get going.

What Is Python and What Can You Do With It?

As I've mentioned, the Python programming language is an excellent programming language for beginners. Python is designed so that it is easy to read by people. The way that Python is laid out and the commands it uses all make it straightforward to read and understand.

You can do some amazing things with Python. Here are just some of the many things it is used for:

- Making windows with buttons and text fields
- Creating computer games
- Making animations
- Building websites

- Analysing scientific data
- Hacking computers

Who Should Read This Book?

Adventures in Python is for any young person who has an interest in making things happen on a computer. You might perhaps be unsure of how to get started or want to develop your current skills further. Whatever your reasons, this book will be your guide for a journey with Python. Your adventures will take you from installing Python, through learning the basics of programming, to discovering how to create your own project. By the end of your adventures you will have acquired the skills you need to create whatever you want!

What You Will Learn

With this book you will discover some of the amazing things you can do with Python. You'll learn about the fundamental programming concepts needed to design and make your own programs.

The Python projects in this book are arranged in adventures. All the projects in an adventure are grouped by a similar topic. For example, in Adventure 7 you'll create several programs that show you how to use the mouse with your Python programs.

The programming concepts you'll learn include Python code that enables your programs to make decisions, allows your programs to repeat complex tasks in a short amount of time and a whole lot more. By building on top of these concepts in your adventures you'll also develop graphical user interfaces, animations and games.

What You Will Need
for the Projects

Python is a programming language that is **cross-platform**. This means that it can run on computers with different **operating systems**. For example, you can write a program on a computer that runs Windows 7 and it will also work on an Apple Mac. There are a couple of slight differences in the way that Python works on different operating systems, but you won't come across these in this book, and they aren't that common.

An **operating system** is software that allows your computer to do its basic functions, such as allowing you to use mice and keyboards on the computer, save files and connect to the Internet. Microsoft Windows and Mac OS X are two examples of operating systems.

A **cross-platform** programming language works on computers with different operating systems. This means you can write a program on one computer and it will work on most other computers.

Another benefit of Python being cross-platform is that you can use this book whether you use Windows, Mac or Linux—the programs will work just the same on all of them.

So, all you need for your adventures is a computer running Windows, Mac or Linux, an Internet connection, a mouse, keyboard and computer monitor. That's it! You don't need anything else.

CRAIG SAYS:

Although it is possible to run Python on Android tablet computers, not all of the things covered in this book are available on a tablet. It's not currently possible to complete most of the adventures with a tablet or phone.

How This Book Is Organised

This book contains Python programs that teach you the basics of the Python programming language and the different things it can do. As you're led through some really fun and creative programs, you'll learn how to use Python.

Adventure 1 introduces Python and shows you how to create programs that use text. You'll create some cool programs, like a control panel for an imaginary spaceship. In Adventure 2, you'll create drawings using Python's built-in `turtle` module. You'll make pictures and build on the things you learned about Python in Adventure 1.

Adventures 3 and 4 introduce you to making programs that use graphical interfaces that include familiar things like buttons, text boxes and sliders.

From the Adventure 5 onwards, you'll be introduced to the `PyGame` library for Python. The `PyGame` library makes it easier to do a wide range of things with Python, including making computer games of your own. You'll find instructions on how to install `PyGame` in the Appendix.

In Adventure 5, you'll use some of `PyGame`'s features to draw shapes and make animations, and in Adventure 6 you'll find out how to use `PyGame` to detect keyboard presses for input in your programs, allowing you to take control of what happens when the program runs. In Adventure 7, you'll learn how to use the mouse with your programs.

Adventure 8 shows you how to use images in your `PyGame` program and guides you through a series of fun programs, including controlling a character to walk across the window using the keyboard. In Adventure 9, you'll learn how to use sounds and music with `PyGame` so you can add music and sounds to your games.

Adventure 10 takes you on a final, big adventure in which you will combine many of the things you learned in your earlier adventures to create a game in which two players compete to collect coins. The game wraps up what you've learned–all in a single program. Through your adventures, you'll learn a lot about programming.

Time to get going!

Setting Up Python

This section will show you how to set up Python on your computer. Choose the section that matches your operating system (OS) to get started.

Windows 8

Microsoft Windows 8 is an operating system that is widely used all over the world. At the time this book is being written, Windows 8 is the operating system that is on most new computers. If you're using Windows 8 on your computer, follow these instructions to install Python.

Installing

Installing Python on Windows 8 is quite straightforward. Follow these steps to install it:

1. Open a web browser (such as Internet Explorer, Chrome or Firefox).
2. In the web browser, click in the address bar.
3. Type this text into the address bar: python.org/downloads.
4. Press the Enter key on the keyboard.
5. When the page loads, click on Download Python 2.7.8 (sometimes the file will download when you click this link, if it does skip Step 6).
6. Scroll down to the Download section and click on Windows x86 MSI Installer (see Figure I-2).
7. When the file has downloaded, open it.
8. When the installer window opens, select Install for all users and click next.
9. Click next again.
10. Click next a third time!
11. When asked if you want the program to install software on your computer, click Yes.
12. Wait for it to install.
13. Once it is installed, click Finish (see Figure I-3).
14. Python is now installed on your computer.

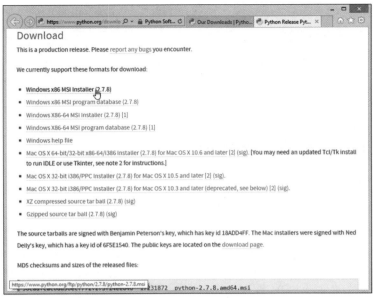

FIGURE I-2 Downloading Python for Windows 8

FIGURE I-3 Python has been installed on Windows 8.

Opening

Now that Python is installed, you can open it. IDLE is a program that allows you to run, make and edit Python programs. It includes lots of helpful features to make creating programs straightforward. Remember these steps to open Python with IDLE as you'll need them throughout your adventures.

To open IDLE, follow these steps:

1. Press the Windows key on your keyboard.

2. Type **IDLE** and select the Idle (Python GUI) option. IDLE is one of the ways you can use Python on your computer, and the program has many features that help you when you write your programs.

3. IDLE will now open—you are ready to start using Python (see Figure I-4)! It's time to try your first program, so skip to "Creating Your First Program" at the end of this chapter.

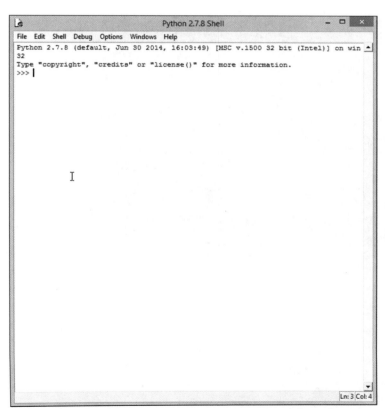

FIGURE I-4 IDLE installed and Python opened on Windows 8

Windows 7

Despite not being the most recent version of Windows, Microsoft Windows 7 is still very widely used. All the screenshots in this book were taken on Windows 7. If your computer uses Windows 7, here's how to install Python.

Installing

Follow these step-by-step instructions to install Python on Windows 7:

1. Open a web browser (such as Internet Explorer, Chrome or Firefox).

2. In the address bar, type www.python.org/downloads to go to the Downloads page on the Python website.

3. Once the page has loaded, click on the button labeled Download Python 2.7.8 (Figure I-5). Sometimes the file will download when you click this link, if it does skip Step 4.

FIGURE I-5 Downloading Python for Windows 7

4. Scroll down to the Download section and click on Windows x86 MSI Installer.

5. Wait for the file to download, then go to your `Downloads` folder and double-click on the `python-2.7.8.msi` file.

6. A dialog box might appear asking if you are sure you want to run the program. If this happens, click the Run button to continue.

7. The installer will ask you if you want to install Python for all users on the computer, or just the current user. Choose the option to Install For All Users, and click Next.

8. Click Next again . . . and again!

9. A dialog box will appear asking if you want to allow the file to make changes to your computer. Click Yes.

10. Python will now install on your computer. Wait until this finishes before doing anything else.

11. Once the installation completes (see Figure I-6), click Finish and follow the steps in the next section to open Python.

FIGURE I-6 Python has been installed on Windows 7.

Opening

IDLE is the name of a program that allows you to run, make and edit Python programs. It includes lots of helpful features to make creating programs straightforward. Remember these steps to open Python with IDLE as you'll need them throughout your adventures:

1. You can open Python from the Start menu. Click the Start button in the bottom-left corner of the screen.

2. Click on All Programs to bring up the list of programs installed on your computer.

3. Select the `Python 2.7` folder to show all the options for using Python. The list of programs should be in alphabetical order.

4. Click on the IDLE (Python GUI) icon in the start menu. IDLE is one of the ways you can use Python on your computer, and the program has many features that help you when you write your programs.

5. Wait for IDLE to open (see Figure 1-7). Congratulations! You are ready to start using Python! It's time to try your first program, so skip to "Creating Your First Program" at the end of this chapter.

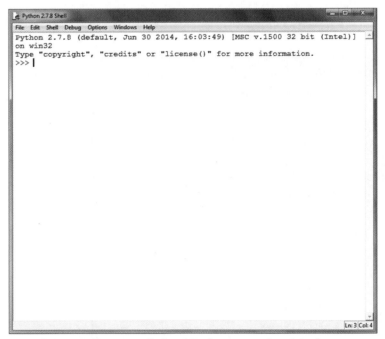

FIGURE 1-7 IDLE installed and Python opened on Windows 7

Mac OS X

The operating system that comes with Apple Mac computers is Mac OS X. There are many different versions of this operating system, and any version of Mac OS X after and including 10.6 will work with these installation instructions. To install Python on your Mac, follow the instructions in this section.

Installing

Follow these steps to install Python on your computer:

1. Open a web browser (such as Safari, Chrome or Firefox).

2. In the address bar, type www.python.org/download and press the Enter key to go to the Download page for Python.

3. Click on the button that says Download Python 2.7.8 (sometimes the file will download when you click this link, if it does skip Step 4).

4. When the page has loaded, scroll down to find the `Python 2.7.8 Mac OS X 64-bit/32-bit x86-64/i386` file. Click on it to download it (see Figure 1-8). Be a bit careful here—there are several versions of Python listed, so make sure you click on the one that that says Python 2.7.8 and Mac.

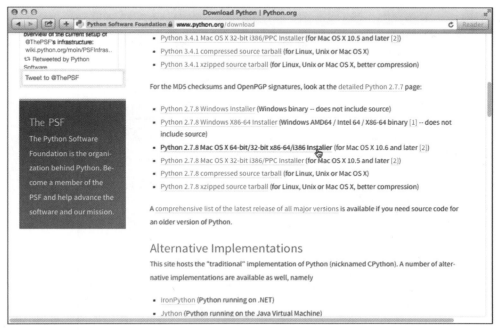

FIGURE I-8 Downloading Python for Mac OS X

Don't download Python 3! There are two versions of Python that are commonly used, Python 2.7 and Python 3. Some of the software used in your adventures only support Python 2.7, so make sure you don't download Python 3.

5. When the file has downloaded, click on the Finder icon and go to your `Downloads` folder.

6. Find the file you just downloaded. It should be called `python-2.7.8-macosx10.6.dmg`.

7. Double-click on the file to open it.

8. Right-click on `Python.mpkg` and click on Open With⇨Installer (see Figure I-9).

FIGURE I-9 Installing Python on a Mac

9. When asked if you want to open it, click Open. Then click Continue three times and then click Agree.

10. Next, click Install and when prompted type in your password and click Install Software.

11. Wait while Python installs.

12. When the installation completes (see Figure I-10) you can now use Python on your computer. (It's also a good idea to remove the installer that you no longer need.) Click Close.

FIGURE I-10 Python has been installed on the Mac

13. On the desktop, right-click on the Python 2.7.8 disk image and select Eject.

Opening

IDLE is the name of a program that allows you to run, make and edit Python programs. It includes lots of helpful features to make creating programs straightforward. These steps show you how to open IDLE. Remember these steps, as you will be using them throughout the book:

1. Open a new finder window and click on the `Applications` folder on the sidebar to show all the applications installed on your computer.

2. In the list of installed applications, find Python 2.7. Double-click on Python 2.7 to open the folder.

3. Double-click on IDLE. Wait until IDLE loads. IDLE is one of the ways you can use Python on your computer, and the program has many features that help you when you write your programs.

If you get a WARNING about Tcl/Tk being unstable, just ignore it.

4. When IDLE has loaded, you're ready to start using Python (see Figure I-11)! It's time to try your first program, so skip to "Creating Your First Program" at the end of this chapter.

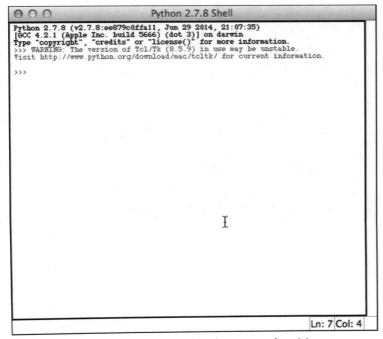

FIGURE I-11 IDLE installed and Python opened on Mac

Linux (Ubuntu)

Operating systems that are based on Linux are free to install and use on your computer. There are many different distributions of Linux, each with its own unique flavour. For this set of instructions, I've chosen to show you how to install Python on the Ubuntu 14.04 distribution. These instructions should work on most other distributions, though you might find they don't work on all of them.

Installing

Ubuntu 14.04 comes with Python 2.7 pre-installed. Despite this, you still need to install IDLE. IDLE is the name of a program that allows you to run, make and edit Python programs. It includes lots of helpful features to make creating programs straightforward. Follow these steps to install IDLE for Python 2.7:

1. Click on the Dash button, or press the super key, to open the Ubuntu dashboard.

2. In the search box of the dashboard, type **terminal** and click on the Terminal program to open it.

3. Once the Terminal is open, type in the following:

   ```
   apt-get update && sudo apt-get upgrade
   ```

4. Press Enter and type in your password if asked (see Figure I-12). Wait for a bit while the update takes place. Type in **Y** and press Enter if asked.

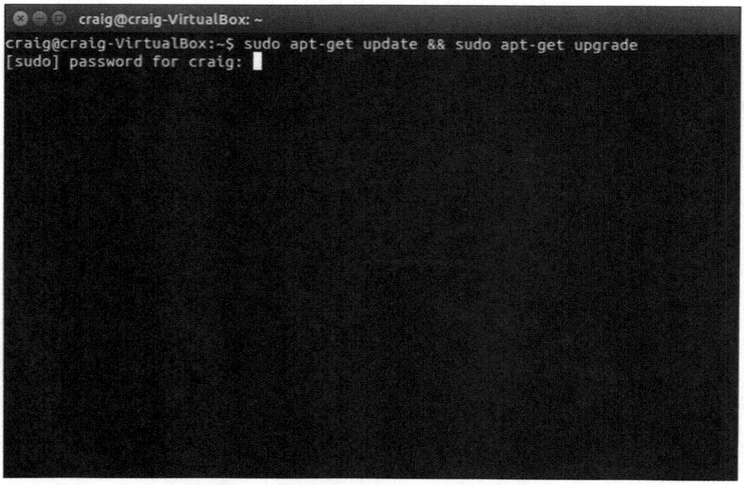

FIGURE I-12 The installation process in Linux

5. Wait for the upgrades to install. When this is complete, type in the following to install IDLE (see Figure I-13):

```
sudo apt-get install idle-python2.7
```

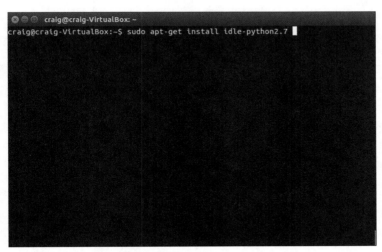

FIGURE I-13 Installing IDLE on Linux

6. If you are asked if you want to continue, type **Y** and press Enter.

7. Wait while IDLE installs. IDLE is one of the ways you can use Python on your computer, and the program has many features that help you when you write your programs. When this finishes, you are ready to open IDLE to write and run Python programs on your computer.

Opening

The next steps show you how to open IDLE. Remember these steps, as you will use them throughout your adventures:

1. Click on the Dash icon to open the dashboard.

2. In the search field, type **IDLE** and click on the IDLE icon when it is found.

3. IDLE will now open—you are ready to start using Python (see Figure I-14)! It's time to try your first program, so skip to "Creating Your First Program" at the end of this chapter.

FIGURE I-14 IDLE installed and Python opened on Linux

Raspberry Pi

The Raspberry Pi is a small, low-cost computer that is great for teaching people how to program. Python was the main language chosen for the Raspberry Pi when it was first developed, and many of the Raspberry Pi's features are designed to use Python.

Installing

If you have a Raspberry Pi, you're lucky—Python is already installed on the Raspberry Pi by default on the main Raspbian operating system, so you don't have to do anything to install it!

There are two versions of Python on the Raspberry Pi: Python 2.7 and Python 3. This book uses Python 2.7 so make sure you choose that one.

Opening

Make sure you have Raspbian installed on your SD card before following these instructions. There are a few different ways you can use Python on the Raspberry Pi. The simplest way is to use IDLE.

To open IDLE:

1. Switch on your Raspberry Pi. You can find guides by searching online if you're not sure how to do this.

2. When asked for your username, type **pi** and then type the password **raspberry**.

3. After logging on, type **startx** to start the desktop.

4. Once the desktop has loaded, you can open IDLE. On the desktop you will see IDLE and IDLE 3. Double-click on IDLE—don't touch IDLE 3! IDLE 3 is for a different version of Python that you won't be using in this book. IDLE is one of the ways you can use Python on your computer, and the program has many features that help you when you write your programs.

5. IDLE may take some time to load, so be patient. The Raspberry Pi is a lot slower than most other computers.

6. When IDLE is open, you are ready to start using Python! It's time to try your first program, so move on to "Creating Your First Program" at the end of this chapter.

Creating Your First Program

Now that you have Python installed on your computer, let's test it out with two short programs. This first program doesn't do much. All it does is display a message. Even so, it's one of the most useful things you can learn, and you can combine it with other things to do a lot.

Time to write your first program. Here's how:

1. Open IDLE. If you're not sure how to do this, look at the instructions for your operating system earlier in this introduction.

2. When IDLE loads, it will open the Python shell. The **shell** is a space where you can type in commands for your Python programs, one line at a time. You can tell that you are using the shell because each line starts with a >>>. This is called the **command prompt**.

DEFINITIONS

The **python shell** is a program that allows you to input one Python statement to be run at a time.

A **command prompt** indicates that the computer is ready to receive commands from the user. The Python command prompt looks like this: >>> It allows you to input a Python command to be performed.

3. Here is your first command for the Python shell. It may not do that much but every adventure starts with one small step! This command (`print`) will display whatever you write in quotation marks after it. Start by placing your cursor after the >>> at the start of the first line and type in this command:

```
print "Time for some adventures"
```

CRAIG SAYS...

Make sure you use double quotation marks around the text. If you use single quotation marks or two apostrophes instead, the program won't work.

4. Press Enter.

5. The `print` command is used to display text on the next line of the Python shell. So, after you press the Enter key, the text you put in the speech marks should appear on the next line of the Python shell (see Figure I-15). In Python, bits of text are called **strings**. Whatever is inside the string between the quotation marks will appear on the next line. Try changing the message in the string to whatever you want. For example, you could change it to your name.

DEFINITIONS

A **string** is a collection of characters—in other words, a piece of text. Strings are used to store letters, symbols and numbers together.

This program is straightforward, but probably not that impressive. With only a slight change you can do so much more.

CRAIG SAYS...

The different bits of the programs in this introduction will be explained in the coming adventures. For now, the important thing is for you to get some hands-on experience with Python.

FIGURE I-15 After you press the Enter key, the text inside the speech marks appears on the next line of the Python shell

This next program builds on the previous one. Instead of displaying a single message on the screen, it displays an infinite number of messages. Follow these steps:

1. Open IDLE if it is not already open.

2. Click in the shell after the command prompt (>>>). Type this line:

    ```
    while True: print "Time for some adventures"
    ```

3. Press the Enter key twice and see what happens (see Figure I-16). Within a short space of time, the phrase "Time for some adventures" should appear on every line of the shell. New lines will be added several times every second. This is because the `while True` part of the command you typed makes the `print` command repeat forever! You'll learn more about this during your adventures later in the book.

4. But how do you stop the command from repeating? Go to the menu at the top of the shell and select Shell⇨Restart Shell. Try changing the program to display whatever you want.

Great work! You've completed your first two programs with Python.

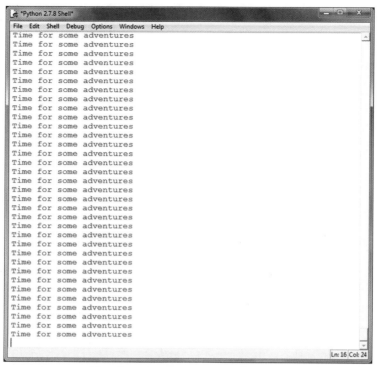

FIGURE I-16 The phrase appears on every line of the shell

The Companion Website

Throughout this book, you'll find references to the *Adventures in Python* companion website, www.wiley.com/go/adventuresinpython. (It's a good idea to bookmark that site now, so you can return to it whenever you need to.) The website includes video tutorials to help you out if you get stuck, code files for some of the more extensive projects and a list of links to locations to download any applications you need during your journey.

Conventions

Throughout the book, there are notes to guide and support you. They use the following key:

Explanations of new or complex computing concepts or terms.

Hints to make life easier.

These are "gotchas" that you should be aware of and avoid during your Python adventures.

Quick quizzes for you to test your understanding or make you think more about the topic.

Important notes from the author that you should be aware of when completing a step or tutorial.

Throughout the book, you will also find two sets of sidebars. *Challenge* sidebars ask you how you might expand on the projects in the book to make changes or add new features. *Digging into the Code* sidebars explain some of the special syntax or programming language, to give you a better understanding of the computer language. When you see this arrow in the code (↵), that means you should type the multiple code lines as one long line in Python. The code is too long to fit on one line in this book, but should be entered as one line in Python.

Reaching Out

There are many great resources available that you might find interesting and useful along your adventures with Python:

- The official Python website (www.python.org) is a great place to find out more about the Python programming language. It also has very extensive documentation, which is super-useful when you're writing your own programs.

- Codecademy (www.codecademy.com) has an excellent online Python tutorial that you can use to test your knowledge of the language.

- Adafruit's blog (www.adafruit.com/blog) and learning site (https://learn.adafruit.com) are excellent places to find inspiration for your Python programs. Although the site mainly deals with electronics, there are plenty of projects that use Python programming and other programming languages to control things. Also, if you have a Raspberry Pi, it is the best place online to learn how to use your Raspberry Pi.

- Full Stack Python (www.fullstackpython.com) is an excellent place for beginners to hone their skills and knowledge. Once you've completed the adventures in this book, this website has an excellent list of other tutorials you can try with Python, along with other useful programming information.

- Python Weekly (www.pythonweekly.com) is a weekly newsletter that showcases Python tutorials, projects and news. Although some of it may be a bit complex for beginners, you can find lots of interesting tutorials, such as creating your own games and animations.

- Effbot (www.effbot.org/tkinterbook/) has excellent documentation for the `Tkinter` library, which is used in some of the adventures in this book. Once you've completed this book, you might find this website really useful for creating your own programs.

- `PyGame`'s official documentation (www.pygame.org/docs/) is a great place to find out more about the `PyGame` library. Not only does it include details of all the features of `PyGame`, but it also has lots of sample projects that show you how other people have used `PyGame` in their programs.

If you would like to contact the author directly, drop him an email at arghbox@gmail.com.

Time to start your adventures!

Adventure 1
Diving into Python

YOU HAVE TRIED two basic Python programs when you set up your computer, but your real journey with Python starts here. Learning to program is a fun and powerful way to control computers. In the adventures in this book, you'll learn the fundamentals of programming with Python and have a lot of fun as you travel through them. You'll create pictures, games and a load of other great stuff. Best of all, you'll develop skills and knowledge of the Python programming language, which you can go on to use to bring your own ideas to life!

On your Python programming journey, you'll discover a new language, a new way to be creative and a new way to solve problems. In this adventure, you'll start by learning some fundamentals and developing a solid foundation. In future chapters, you will revisit all the fundamentals you learn in this chapter and build on them to strengthen your ability as a programmer.

The screenshots shown throughout the book were taken on a computer running Windows 7.

You may not be using a computer running Windows 7, of course. It's not a problem if you are using a different sort of computer as Python is designed to be used on a wide variety of computers, no matter what the operating system is. All of the Python code in this book has been tested to work on Windows, Mac and Linux. The screenshots in this book may look a bit different from what you see in front of you, but there is no difference in the code.

By the end of this adventure you'll already have travelled a long way. You will understand the importance of sequencing in programming and using input and output in Python. You'll have covered the basics of `if` statements and `while` loops, both of which you will use a lot in later adventures. And you will have created a control console for a spaceship to help you launch into your next adventures! Don't be alarmed—that may sound a lot to digest for a beginner but you'll take it one step at a time and it's much easier than it sounds.

What Is Programming?

First things first: before you start your adventures with Python programming it's a good idea for you to be clear about what programming actually is.

Put simply, **programming** is controlling a computer by giving it a set of instructions so that it can perform a particular task.

DEFINITIONS

Programming is using a set of instructions to tell a computer how to perform a task. These instructions are written in programming language. There are many different programming languages; Python, Java, Ruby and C++ are just a few of them.

All of the programs and applications (known as apps) on computers have to be written by people, who use programming languages, such as Python, to tell the computer how to behave when it runs the programs. For example, the web browser you use to visit websites is a program that has been programmed by people, as are the games on your computer, the text messaging app on your phone and even the operating system that runs when you switch your computer on.

CRAIG SAYS...

Your phone is actually a computer. Even your television, washing machine, car and digital clock have computers in them. You may not realise it, but computers are all around us and are increasingly important for our everyday lives. All of these computers run programs and, with the ability to program, you have the potential to create, understand and control these devices that are all around us. Many different languages are used to write programs. In these adventures, you'll be learning to use the Python programming language. Python is known for being good for beginners to use because it is relatively easy to read and also because there are lots of extra bits—known as modules—that can be added to it to allow it do all sorts of exciting things. In this book, you'll use Python version 2.7, as it has better support for computer games programming.

The programming concepts that you learn with Python are common to nearly every programming language. This means that, once you've learned Python, you'll find it easier and faster to learn other programming languages.

Opening IDLE

In order to use Python you'll need to open an application on your computer that can run Python. One of the applications used for writing and editing Python programs is called IDLE, and this is installed by default when you install Python. If you haven't already installed Python, do so now—you will find instructions on how to do this in the introduction. Check carefully that you install Python 2.7, and not Python 3, as there are some slight differences between them.

Done? Good—now you can open IDLE. The way you do this varies slightly depending on system you're using:

- On **Windows 7**, select Start➪All Programs➪IDLE.
- On **Windows 8.1**, press the Windows key on your keyboard, type IDLE to search for the program and double-click IDLE when it has been found.
- On **Mac**, select Finder➪Applications➪IDLE.
- On **Raspberry Pi**, select Start➪Programming➪IDLE.
- On **Ubuntu Linux**, select Launch➪IDLE.

Once IDLE is open you should see a window that looks something like Figure 1-1.

FIGURE 1-1 IDLE is ready for you to start programming!

IDLE is an **Integrated Development Environment**, or **IDE** for short. This means that it not only lets you write code but also includes a useful set of features for running, testing and editing your programs. In fact, you could write your programs in a basic text editor, such as Notepad, but the extra features of an IDE make it easier to manage your programs. There are many different IDEs available for Python, such as Eclipse, Geany, NINJA IDE and a whole load more. IDLE is a good IDE for starters, but as you go along you might want to try out other IDEs that have more features that support you when you're programming.

Integrated Development Environments (IDEs) are programs designed to help you develop your programs. They let you write, edit and save your programs just like a regular text editor, but also include other features for testing, debugging and running your programs.

Returning to Your First Python Program

In the introduction to this book, you created two short Python programs. You completed them to quickly see some examples of what Python can do. In this section, you'll return to the first of these programs to understand what it is doing and how you can change it to use in it your own programs.

Once IDLE is open, that's it! You can start giving commands to Python. At the beginning of the bottom line, you'll notice there are >>> characters. These mean that IDLE is waiting for you to tell it what to do (see Figure 1-2). The >>> is called the **command prompt** as it is prompting you to give it an instruction or command.

The window into which you type the commands is called a **python shell**. It takes one command at a time and runs it before you can type the next line. A single line of Python code is called a **statement**, although you will see later that some statements can be more than one line long.

A **statement** is a single instruction of Python code. Statements are usually one line long, though some special statements can be several lines long. Statements are like a sentence in English and contain all the information Python needs to carry out a certain instruction, such as print a string or add two numbers together.

Place your cursor after the command prompt and type the following statement:

```
print "Hello world!"
```

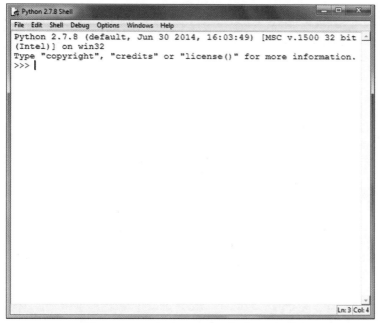

FIGURE 1-2 The command prompt in a Python shell

Press Enter and the `"Hello world!"` message will be displayed, as shown in Figure 1-3.

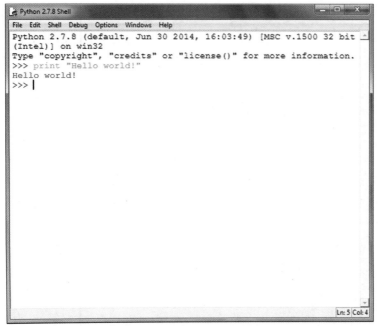

FIGURE 1-3 Your first Python program running in the Python shell

You can type whatever you like between the speech (quote) marks. Whenever you use the `print` instruction, whatever text you enter is displayed in the IDLE shell. The text inside the quote marks is called a **string**.

Try changing your message by typing different words between the quote marks. You could try changing the `print` statement to display your name in the IDLE shell, for example by typing:

```
print "Hello Ellen!"
```

It Isn't Working—Grrr!

There will be times when you will find yourself jumping up and down in frustration, wondering why your program doesn't work. It's best to cover this now rather than waiting until later in the book, so you know what to do when this happens—because it will happen!

If your program doesn't work, it means you have made a mistake in the instructions you have typed in. Let's go through some common mistakes you can make. You'll still make them—everyone does!—but if you know what mistakes you might have made it means you'll know what to look for when your program doesn't work as intended.

In an IDLE shell, type the following line after the command prompt and press Enter:

```
Print "I like trains"
```

What happens? You get an error message like the one in Figure 1-4. Can you work out why this happened?

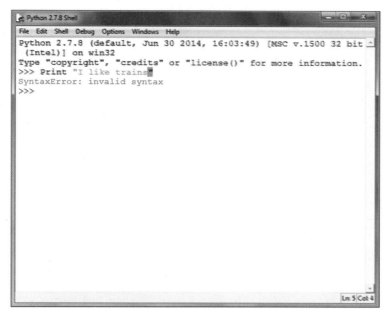

FIGURE 1-4 An error message in the Python shell

Python expects things to be written in a certain way and capitalisation is extremely important for Python. So, for example, if you capitalise any letter in the `print` command, Python will get confused.

Although you know what you want the computer to do, computers aren't actually all that clever. They have to be given very precise instructions; if your instructions aren't in exactly the right form, your computer can't guess what you really meant. That's why you have to stick to the rules of the programming language in order for the computer to understand you. These language rules are called **syntax**. When you don't stick to the rules of the syntax, you get a **syntax error** like the one in Figure 1-4.

Syntax is the set of rules about structure that a programming language must follow in order to work. Syntax is like the spelling and grammar in spoken and written language.

Syntax errors happen when you break the syntax rules of a programming language. If you don't follow the syntax rules, the computer will not understand what you are trying to do, because it takes instructions literally and cannot guess what you mean if your syntax isn't quite right.

Errors are also called bugs. The process of finding and fixing bugs in your code is called debugging. Let's have some debugging practice. Here are some other pieces of code with syntax errors in them. What are the bugs in this code and how would you fix them?

```
pirnt "Something"
print 'Cakes"
print Beep
print Sharks"
 print "Shakes"
```

Found them? Here are the bugs in order:

1. `print` is spelled incorrectly. You can fix the error simply by fixing the spelling of the command.

2. The speech marks do not match; one is single and one is double.

3. The speech marks are missing, therefore Python doesn't know that you meant to create a string.

4. The opening speech mark is missing.

5. There is a space at the start of the line. Did you spot that?

Debugging is a skill in itself. Everyone makes mistakes but being able to find and correct your mistakes is what will make you into a great programmer. Take your time when you start; it may be frustrating to see error messages, but it is a great feeling when you fix a problem.

Using a File Editor

VIDEO

For a video that walks you through the steps of using a File Editor, visit the companion website at www.wiley.com/go/adventuresinpython. Click the Videos tab and select the appropriate file.

The IDLE shell is great for trying out bits of Python code quickly, but it can be very time consuming when you have to write out your code one line at a time, every time you want to use it.

Using a **file editor** in IDLE, instead of the interactive shell, enables you to create programs with many lines of code. It also allows you to save these programs so that you can use them again and again. Another advantage of the file editor is that it waits for you to tell it to run the program, unlike the shell, which runs a program whenever you end a statement. The following steps guide you through writing a program using a file editor.

A **file editor** allows you to create, save and modify programs that contain several lines of Python statements. Unlike a Python shell, there is no command prompt so each statement will not automatically run when you press Enter. Instead, the program will run lines of code in sequence—but not until you tell it to.

1. Open the file editor in IDLE by selecting File⇨New Window (this may be called New File in some versions of IDLE). A new IDLE window will appear. This will look something like Figure 1-5.

FIGURE 1-5 The IDLE file editor window

You might notice that there is no command prompt (>>>) at the start of the line. You might also notice that when you press Enter it does not run your code. Don't panic! This is what is supposed to happen.

2. Let's make the most of being able to create programs across several lines—such luxury. Type the following code into the file editor:

```
print "Space:"
print "A really big place"
print "that contains a lot of stuff"
print "and a lot of nothing between the stuff."
print "This is why it is called space."
```

3. To run the program, select Run⇨Run Module from the menu at the top of the window.

4. When you are asked if it is OK to save, click Yes. Create a folder called Adventure 1 and save your file as space.py.

After a short while, the Python shell will appear and the message will be printed to it.

When you save the file, make sure you include .py at the end of the filename. Some versions of IDLE don't include this automatically.

Another major benefit of the file editor is that, unlike the shell, you can change your programs and then rerun them. You're going to try that now.

Click on the file editor again. Remember that the file editor doesn't have a command prompt (>>>) and that's how you can tell the difference between the shell and the file editor.

Add the following lines of code to what you've already written:

```
print ""
print "This definition of space is stupid."
```

Run the program again (choose Run⇨Run Module) and the changes to the program will be included in the output, as shown in Figure 1-6. Notice that the line with the empty speech marks (" ") prints out a blank line.

So far in Python you've written commands in the shell and the file editor, and used the print statement to output text onto the shell. Next you'll find out how to change what your program does by inputting different strings when you run it.

FIGURE 1-6 The completed program and output in IDLE

You can download the completed `space.py` code file and other code in this chapter from the companion website at www.wiley.com/go/adventuresinpython— but you will learn more by typing in the code yourself as you work through the steps.

Asking Questions with Variables

For a video that walks you through the steps of asking a question using variables, visit the companion website at www.wiley.com/go/adventuresinpython. Click the Videos tab and select the appropriate file.

In the last example, you used the `print` statement to display strings in the IDLE shell. The strings didn't change each time you ran the program. But how would you like to be able to change the program every time it runs? For example, you could have the program address each user by name. You are now going to do this by using two new things in Python: **variables** and the `raw_input()` **function**. You'll learn more about variables and functions shortly but, to get started, try this example:

1. In IDLE, open a new file editor window by clicking File⇨New Window.

2. Type in this code, exactly as it is shown here, including the spaces:

```
yourName = raw_input("What is your name? ")
print "Hello " + yourName
```

3. Now run the program by clicking Run⇨Run Module. Save your program as `question.py` in the `Adventure 1` folder, which you created in the previous exercise.

4. When the Python shell appears, the question `What is your name?` should be displayed, as shown in Figure 1-7.

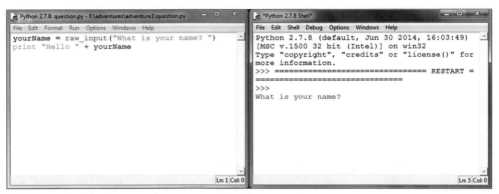

FIGURE 1-7 The command prompt waiting for you to input a name

5. Type your name after the question and press Enter. (Don't press Enter immediately without typing a name—if you do that, the program will not do what you want it to do.)

6. The computer will say hello to you; for example, it will print (or "output") `Hello Ellen`.

7. To run the program again, select the File Editor window and click on Run⇨Run Module.

The + sign between the `Hello` string and the `yourName` string variable joins these two strings together. This is called string **concatenation**. The + sign is necessary for joining the two string values.

Concatenation is when a program combines two or more strings together to make a new string.

A **variable** stores a value so that it can be reused later in a program. All variables have a name and a value. Variable names are used to identify the variable. The value of the variable can be a number, a string, a list of items and a few other things.

A **function** is a reusable bit of code. It can be reused without needing to rewrite the contents of the function. Instead, you call the function by using its name and any **arguments** it requires. It is possible to write your own function.

An **argument** is a value that is passed to a function. The value of the argument can change how the function runs.

Run the program again, but this time enter a different name when the computer asks you what your name is. Is the output different? What happens if you input a word that isn't a name? What happens if you input a sentence?

A Bit About Variables

Variables are super-useful. They store values so that you can reuse them later. This makes your programs more manageable as you don't have to change loads of lines of code whenever you just want to change a single value.

DIGGING INTO THE CODE

The `raw_input()` function allows the user to input strings when prompted, which the program can use to change the values of variables that the Python program uses while it is running. The preceding example asks what your name is. The output for the program will change based on the name you input. For example if you input `Jonesie`, it would output `Hello Jonesie`.

A variable stores a value, which can be reused and changed. In the preceding example, `yourName` is a variable, which stores the result of `raw_input()`. Storing a variable is different from saving it. When you store it, the value of the variable is stored temporarily while the program is being used in the computer's short-term memory. As soon as you close the program or restart the computer, the value of the variable in memory is lost. When you save something, however, it means it is stored almost permanently, even after the program is closed. So remember that storing a variable is not the same thing as saving it.

For example, when you use someone's name in a long program, it makes more sense to use a string variable, instead of writing the name out in a new string every time. Using a variable means that when you want to change the name of the person using the program you only need to change the value of the variable instead of changing it every time the name appears in the program.

You write variables using a name, an equals sign and a value. You can name the variable almost anything you want, although it is a good idea to call it something that clearly describes what it is, so you will remember it easily. In the example you just did, the variable was called `yourName`—but you could have called it anything. You could call it `kittens` if you wanted, and the computer would deal with it in exactly the same way, although it wouldn't make much sense to someone else reading it.

Although you can name variables almost anything you want, avoid using variables that begin with symbols or numbers. For example, `5fingers` is not a valid variable name as it begins with the number 5.

So far, you've created a variable that stores a string value. Variables that store strings can be placed anywhere you would expect a string, including after the `print` statement or as an argument in the `raw_input()` function.

When using variables, it's important to use the right case and spelling when you type it in. If you don't type the name of the variable exactly the same each time you reuse it, you'll get an error message or the program will do something that you didn't expect. It's easy to tell the difference between variables and functions: variables do not have brackets after them; functions do have brackets.

CHALLENGE

Add more questions and responses to your program. For example, your program could ask what the user's favourite animal is, like this:

```
favAnimal = raw_input("What is your favourite ↵
  animal?")
print "I also like " + favAnimal + ", though ↵
  they're not my favourite."
```

Using Variables for a Fill-in-the-Blanks Story

In this part of the adventure, you'll use variables again to create a fill-in-the-blanks story. Using input, your program will include three variables—a name, an object and a place—as details in a mini-story. By using input to change the values for these three variables, you can create a slightly different story every time:

1. Open IDLE and open the file editor with File⇨New Window.

2. For this program, the first thing you will need is a way to get the user to input the name, object and place variables. The following code will do this:

```
personName = raw_input("Enter a name: ")
anObject = raw_input("Enter an object: ")
place = raw_input("Enter a place: ")
```

Notice the space at the end of each string. Python carries out any commands you give it exactly as you type them. This means that if you don't leave a space at the end of the line, there won't be a gap between the prompt and the input.

3. Now you are going to write a story using the variables to represent certain words in the story, which will be stored in the story variable. Add this code to your program:

```
story = personName + " was walking through " + place + ".
" + place + " was not usually very interesting. " +
personName + " spotted a small " + anObject + ". Suddenly
the " + anObject + " jumped up and ran away. " +
personName + " decided not to go to " + place + " again."
```

CRAIG SAYS:

Just look at that code—there are plenty of chances for you to create errors and potentially a very good opportunity for you to test your debugging skills!

Be very careful when you type out this code. Take your time; if you get an error, remember that it's normal for this to happen when you first start learning Python. Finding and correcting errors will really help you to learn! Make sure you remember to include pairs of speech marks around strings, spell variables correctly and use the + symbol to concatenate it all together. If you make any mistakes, it is a perfect opportunity to test your debugging skills.

4. Finally, you're going to output the story using the print statement, by adding this to your program:

```
print story
```

5. Run the program with Run⇨Run Module. Save your file as `story.py` in the `Adventure 1` folder.

6. When the program runs, enter a name, object and location as you are prompted for each (see Figure 1-8). For example:

```
Enter a name: John
Enter an object: pineapple
Enter a place: the kitchen
```

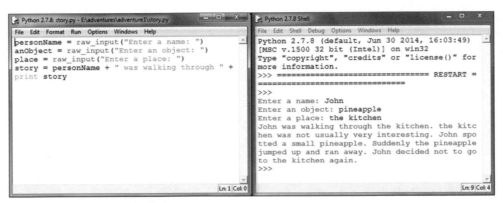

FIGURE 1-8 The finished program

7. Once the program runs, you should see the story with your input included.

CHALLENGE

Write your own story that uses strings, input and variables. You can include as many string variables as you want. Just remember the rules about strings, concatenation and creating variables.

As mentioned earlier in this adventure, variables can be reused several times throughout a program. You can see this in action in this program as `personName`, `place` and `Object` variables are all used several times in the program.

Making the Program Make Decisions: Conditionals

For a video that walks you through the steps of using conditionals, visit the companion website at www.wiley.com/go/adventuresinpython. Click the Videos tab and select the appropriate file.

So far, you've been able to make your programs input and output data. You can do a lot with this, but the output of the programs will still look pretty much the same when you run them. To make your programs even better, you can use `if` statements to make the computer make decisions automatically and change the output depending on certain conditions.

Using if Statements

In this part of the adventure, the Python program will ask Do you have any biscuits?. If the answer is yes then the program will print They look delicious. If the answer is no or anything else, it will print I don't believe you.

1. As usual, you need to open IDLE and create a new file editor window with File⇨New Window (remember, this is New File in some versions of Python).

2. In the file editor, type the following code:

```
hasBiscuits = raw_input("Do you have any biscuits? ")
```

3. Next the program will need to use the `if` statement to check whether the input is yes. If the input is yes, the program will then print They look delicious.

```
if hasBiscuits == "yes":
    print "They look delicious"
```

Make sure you copy the code exactly, including the four spaces at the start of the second line. Python uses four spaces at the start of lines so that it knows which bits of code belong to the `if` statement. For example, if you don't put the four spaces at the start of the `print` line it will always run, making the `if` statement pointless. As a result, Python will send you an error message if you forget the four spaces at the start of the line after an `if` statement. Anything that you want to run outside an `if` statement doesn't need to have four spaces before it, but every bit of code that will only run if the `if` statement is `True` must be indented by four spaces.

The `if` bit tells Python that you want it to check a condition and do something if that is `True`. This is known as an **if statement**. Notice that two equals signs are used to indicate the thing that Python is checking; this is an *equals to* comparison. It will check whether the value of the `hasBiscuits` is yes and, if it is `True`, it will run the `print` bit `"They look delicious"`. If it is not `True`, this bit of code won't run.

If statements are used in Python to change what happens in the program based on a condition. For example, a program could use an `if` statement to check whether someone has input the correct answer, displaying a `correct` message if they're right and `incorrect` if they're wrong.

Take care with the syntax. At the end of the line with the `if` statement is a colon. This colon tells Python that everything following the colon is part of the `if` statement and will run when the value of `hasBiscuits` is yes. To help identify which lines belong to the `if` statement, all lines that follow the colon are indented by four spaces. These spaces are super important—as is everything else you learn. Everything is super important!

Next, you need the code that will run if the answer is not `yes`. To do this you use an **else statement**. An `else` statement is used after an `if` statement. The code it contains will only run if the condition of the `if` statements is not `True`. In this example, it will run when `hasBiscuits` is not `yes`.

An **if statement** is used in programs to decide whether or not to run a section of code. The decision is made based on a condition. Conditions are like questions, for example, "Is the price of the chocolate bar equal to the amount of money given for it?" or "Was the input equal to Yes?". If the condition is `True` then the code in the body of the `if` statement will run; otherwise, it will not.

An **else statement** works alongside an `if` statement. The body of an `if` statement will run only if its condition is `True`. On the other hand, the body of the matching `else` statement will only run if the condition of the `if` statement is `False`.

4. Add the following code to your program. Make sure you don't indent the first line, but do indent the second line by four spaces:

```
else:
    print "I don't believe you"
```

5. Run the program in the usual way by clicking Run➪Run Module. Save this program as `biscuits.py` in the `Adventure 1` folder.

6. Run the program (see Figure 1-9). Type **yes** with a lower case y, and press Enter. What do you think would happen if the y was capitalised?

7. Run the program again and change the input to **no**. What do you think would happen if you input something other than "yes" or "no"? You can see the program running in Figure 1-9.

FIGURE 1-9 The finished program running alongside the Python code

Nested if Statements

Sometimes after getting the answer to one question, you will want to ask a subsequent question. For example, in the last example, the program asked if you had any biscuits. You now want it to ask if it can have a biscuit if the answer is yes.

You can use `if` statements to do this by putting one `if` statement inside another; this is called **nesting** and creates a nested `if` statement. Try it out with this next example.

Nesting is where one `if` statement or loop is located inside of another `if` statement or loop.

CHALLENGE

There is an infinite number of questions you could ask with an `if` statement. Questions like "What is 2 + 2?" and "What is the capital of Assyria?" are good. Create your own quiz with several questions to test the names of capital cities of several countries and use `if` statements to check whether the answers are correct.

1. Open your last program, the one you saved as `biscuits.py` in the Adventure 1 folder.

2. After the line that reads `print "They look delicious"`, add the following Python code (note that the first line is indented by four spaces):

```
willShare = raw_input("Can I have one? ")
if willShare == "yes":
    print "Thank you!"
else:
    print "I guess computers don't eat biscuits anyway..."
```

3. The full program should look like this (see Figure 1-10). Remember to make your indentation match the example code:

```
hasBiscuits = raw_input("Do you have any biscuits? ")
if hasBiscuits == "yes":
    print "They look delicious"
    willShare = raw_input("Can I have one? ")
    if willShare == "yes":
        print "Thank you!"
    else:
        print "I guess computers don't eat biscuits anyway..."
else:
    print "I don't believe you"
```

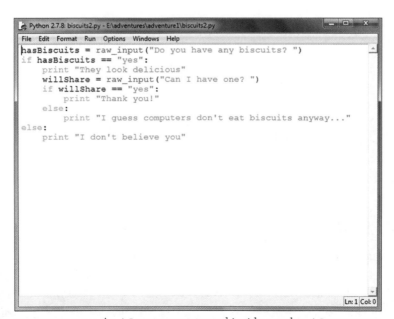

FIGURE 1-10 An `if` statement nested inside another `if` statement

4. Save the program and run it using Run⇨Run Module. When the program runs, it will now ask an extra question if the answer "yes" is given to the first question. You can see this in Figure 1-11.

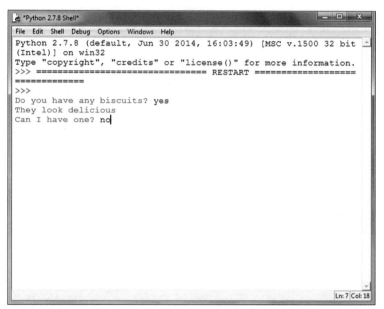

FIGURE 1-11 Replying "yes" to the first question will cause the program to ask a second question.

Creating an Imaginary Vending Machine

To get more practice using conditionals, you are now going to make a program for a vending machine that dispenses food. You'll have to use your imagination here as the program won't actually give you food! For that to happen you'd have to make your program control motors and buy the food. That will all be possible when you know more, but for now you're just trying to write some Python. So on with the program!

To create your imaginary vending machine program, first you'll display a list of choices for the user. Each choice is a type of food that can be ordered from the vending machine:

1. Open IDLE and create a new file with File⇨New Window.

2. In the new window, type the following lines of code to create a list of options:

```
print "a: Cake"
print "b: Carrot"
print "c: Fish"
print "d: Soup"
```

3. Next add a `raw_input()` function that will take the user's option and store it in a `choice` variable:

```
choice = raw_input("Select an option (a, b, c or d): ")
```

4. Now add an `if` statement for when the user selects option `a` (which is cake):

```
if choice == "a":
    print "Here is your cake. Yum!"
```

5. Sometimes you need more than the two options that an `if` and `else` statement gives you. An **elif statement** allows you to include additional options. The following lines of Python give three options that use an `elif` statement. Add these lines of Python to your program:

```
elif choice == "b":
    print "Carrots are orange. Have some."
elif choice == "c":
    print "Fish live in water. Enjoy!"
elif choice == "d":
    print "Today's soup is tomato. Spoons are located
    behind you."
```

Elif statements work alongside `if` statements. `elif` is an abbreviation of else if. Like `if` statements, `elif` statements have their own condition and their code will only run if their condition is `True`. An `elif` statement will also only run if all of the conditions of the `if` and `elif` statements above it are `False`.

6. Finally, add an `else` statement to handle all inputs that aren't `a`, `b`, `c` or `d`. An `else` statement will always come last, after `if` statements and `elif` statements, however it is not mandatory, so you could leave it out. This `else` statement is included as you want to handle invalid options as well as valid options:

```
else:
    print choice + " is not a valid option. Have some air."
```

7. Run your code using Run⇨Run Module (see Figure 1-12). Save it as `vending.py` in the `Adventure 1` folder.

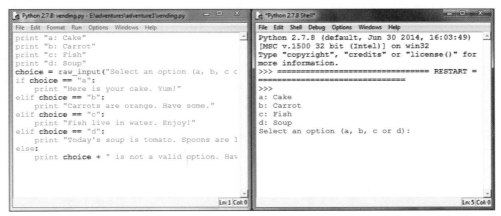

FIGURE 1-12 The finished vending machine code and the Python shell waiting for you to make a choice

Repeating Code with Loops

Until now, every time you wanted to go back to the start you had to rerun your program. You also had to copy and paste code if you wanted it to repeat several times. How inconvenient are you finding that? It wastes time and can make your programs hard to maintain. But never fear—there is a simpler way to do it, by using loops. Loops are a way to make your program repeat blocks of code.

Using while Loops

You're now going to use a `while` loop to create a basic messaging program. This program is so basic that you're effectively sending messages to yourself and no one else.

When the program starts it will ask for a user name. It will then ask the user to input messages, which are then output to the Python shell. The messages will repeat—loop—as long as the input isn't `exit`.

1. Open IDLE and open the file editor with File↭New Window.

2. You first want the program to ask for a user name and store this in the `userName` variable, then ask the user to enter a message. Type this code in your file editor:

```
userName = raw_input("What is your name? ")
message = raw_input("Enter a message: ")
```

3. Next, you'll add a loop to check the user's input and display it. Enter these three lines of Python—these three lines will repeat over and over until the user enters `exit` as an input (see Figure 1-13):

```python
while message != "exit":
    print userName + ": " + message
    message = raw_input("Enter a message: ")
```

4. Run the program with Run⇨Run Module. Save it as `chat.py` in the `Adventure 1` folder.

5. Enter some messages into the program. When you are finished, type `exit` and press Enter.

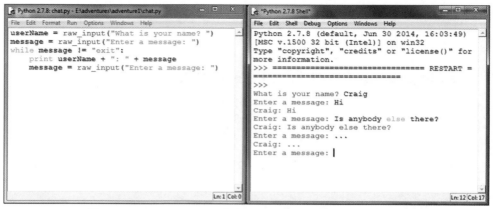

FIGURE 1-13 This program repeats until the user types `exit`.

Remember that indents are important. Put four spaces at the start of each line within the body of the `while` loop.

DIGGING INTO THE CODE

So far, you've used the *equal to* comparator (`==`) in your programs, which checks to see if two values are the same. The *not equal to* comparator (`!=`) is similar, but it checks that two values are not the same. In the example you just completed, the loop will repeat as long as the message input is anything other than `exit`.

While loops are used to repeat a block of code several times. This is a great thing to know how to do. It means you don't have to copy and paste code in order to make it repeat several times. It also means that you can control how many times the block of code repeats, whether that is once, not at all, six times or an infinite number of times.

A **while loop** will repeat a block of code. Like an `if` statement, it has a condition. The loop will only repeat if the condition is `True`. Every time the loop repeats it will check if the condition is `True` or `False`. The loop will stop repeating if the condition changes to `False`.

Infinite while Loops

It's possible to make programs that repeat forever; this is done using a `while` loop. You'll try out this next program in a Python shell as it is only two lines long, but you could also do it in a file editor.

1. Open a Python shell. Remember that a Python shell is distinguishable from a file editor as it has a command prompt (`>>>`) at the start of each line.

2. Copy these two lines of code into the Python shell:

```
while True:
    print "I'm in space!"
```

3. Press Enter. Watch the text scroll infinitely up the screen, as in Figure 1-14.

It can be quite good fun to take over your friend's computer while they're not looking and type this quickly. Change the string in the `print` statement to something like `"I am great"` and watch the message appear hundreds of times before your friend has even noticed what's happening. Of course, you also need to know how to stop the program before violence breaks out. You can stop the loop from repeating by resetting the shell: On the menu bar at the top of the IDLE window, simply click Shell⇨Restart Shell.

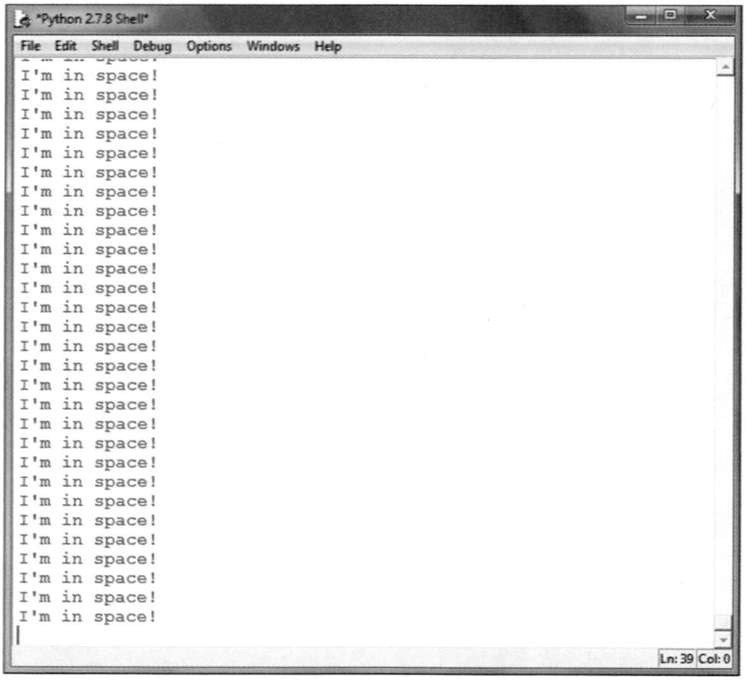

FIGURE 1-14 The loop makes the code repeat infinitely.

Praise Generator

So far, you've done quite a lot in Python, so take a minute to notice how far you've come already, and congratulate yourself. You've learned about input and output, variables, `if`, `else` and `elif` statements, and `while` loops. The flexibility of programming is that you can combine these basic pieces of Python code together in different ways to control what happens.

Let's put it all together. You're now going to combine `if` statements with loops to make a program that gives you praise. You'll use a loop to make the code repeat and an `if` statement to select which praise to output.

1. Create a new file editor by opening IDLE and clicking File⇨New Window.

2. First you'll create a variable called `again`. The first time the program is run this variable is set to `"yes"`, which will mean the loop runs at least once.

   ```
   again = "yes"
   ```

3. Next add the following code to make the program repeat and ask the user what type of praise they would like:

   ```
   while again == "yes":
       praiseType = raw_input("Select a type of praise \n a:
   personality \n b: appearance \n c: intelligence")
   ```

4. The `if` statements are used to respond to the input and output the response:

```python
if praiseType == "a":
    print "You are an interesting person"
elif praiseType == "b":
    print "You are smart"
elif praiseType == "c":
    print "You look good"
else:
    print "That wasn't an option"
```

5. The final line asks the user if they want to continue. Inputting anything other than "yes" will make the program end.

```python
again = raw_input( "Would you like some more praise?")
```

6. Run the program with Run⇨Run Program. Save the program as `praise.py` in the `Adventure 1` folder.

7. When the program runs, choose option a, b or c. The program will loop as long as you type "yes" when asked if you want some more praise (Figure 1-15).

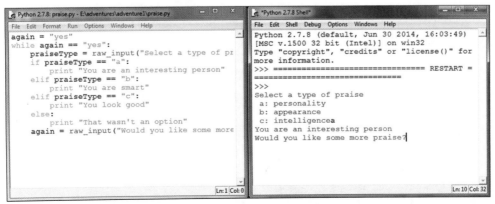

FIGURE 1-15 The program displays a compliment when you enter a, b or c.

A Bigger Adventure: Spaceship Control Console

Spaceships are amazing. They have loads of computer systems to do all sorts of tasks.

There's usually a master computer in a spaceship that controls the other computers. The captain of the ship gives the master computer commands via a console to control everything the ship does.

In the final part of this adventure, you'll build a spaceship command console using all the Python concepts that you've covered in this chapter.

The console will enable your ship to:

- Travel to another planet
- Fire cannons
- Open the airlock
- Self-destruct

On top of that, your command console will be password-protected so that no one can take control of your ship without permission.

Each part of the system will be built in stages so that you can test that it works as you go along.

Set-Up and Password

The first thing you'll do is set up some basic information about the ship.

1. Open IDLE and open the file editor using File➪New Window.

2. Copy the following code into the file editor:

```
import time
shipName = "Nastrama"
captain = "Wallace"
location = "Earth"
password = "Buttercups"
```

You can change the values of these variables to whatever you want, of course. Notice how easy it is to understand what each variable stores, based on its name.

You'll see that you've imported a module called `time`. This is a pre-written module that the program can use, for example, to wait for a number of seconds before proceeding. You'll be using the `time` module later in your program.

A **module** is set of pre-written functions that you can use with your programs. As modules are pre-written, they save you a lot of time as you don't have to write a lot of code yourself, most of which is often quite complex. Anyone can write modules and they enable your programs to do lots of things, from making games to manipulating images.

3. Next it's time to create the password check. Below the variables you just input, add these lines to your code:

```
pAttempt = raw_input("Enter the password: ")
while pAttempt != password:
    print "Password incorrect"
    pAttempt = raw_input("Enter the password: ")
print "Password correct. Welcome to the " + shipName
```

This bit of code will ask the person trying to use the command console to enter the password. If they get it wrong it will keep asking them until they get it right or give up. As soon as they get it right, the program will welcome them to the ship.

4. Save the program as `spaceShipConsole.py` in the `Adventure 1` folder. Click Run⇨Run Module. Test the program to see if the password verification works. If you enter the wrong password it will say `"Password incorrect"`, but if you enter the right password it will welcome you to the ship.

Naturally, the first thing the console will do after the captain has entered the correct password is give some basic information about the ship, including its name and current location. Continue writing your program as follows.

5. Below the code you've written, add the following lines:

```
print ""
print "The spaceship " + shipName + " is currently
  visiting " + location + "."
```

6. Next, you want the program to ask the captain what he or she wants to do and list a set of commands the captain can give the ship:

```
choice = ""
while choice != "/exit":
    print "What would you like to do, " + captain + "?"
    print ""
    print "a. Travel to another planet"
    print "b. Fire cannons"
    print "c. Open the airlock"
    print "d. Self-destruct"
    print "/exit to exit"
    print ""
    choice = raw_input ("Enter your choice: ")
```

7. Save the program and run it using Run⇨Run Module.

8. Enter the correct password. The program should then ask what you want to do, so you need to test whether the four possible choices work—but there's a problem! Whatever input you type in, it won't do anything other than ask you what you want to do again. For now, typing /exit is the only command that will work. When you type /exit the program should finish.

Using the Console to Do Things

When the captain inputs a command the console needs to respond to it—so how do you make that happen? In this section, you'll deal with the commands one at a time.

The "Travel to another planet" command will ask where you want to travel, take a certain amount of time while the ship travels there and then tell you that the ship has arrived.

9. Add this code to your program inside of the while loop:

```
if choice == "a":
    destination = raw_input("Where would you like to
                            go? ")
    print "Leaving " + location
    print "Travelling to " + destination
    time.sleep(5)
    print "Arrived at " + destination
    location = destination
```

10. Next, add the code for the command to fire the cannons:

```python
elif choice == "b":
    print "Firing cannons"
    time.sleep(1)
    print "BANG!"
    time.sleep(1)
```

11. Now add the code for opening the airlock:

```python
elif choice == "c":
    print "Opening airlock"
    time.sleep(3)
    print "Airlock open"
    time.sleep(1)
```

12. Finally, add the code for making the ship self-destruct:

```python
elif choice == "d":
    confirm = raw_input("Are you sure you want
                        the ship to self-destruct?
                        (y/n)")
    if confirm == "y":
        print "Ship will self-destruct in"
        print "3"
        time.sleep(1)
        print "2"
        time.sleep(1)
        print "1"
        time.sleep(1)
        print "Goodbye"
        print "BOOM"
        choice = "/exit"
```

13. You need some code in case the user wants to exit, too:

```python
elif choice == "/exit":
    print "Goodbye"
```

14. Finally, add some code in case the user types something that is not a valid choice:

```python
else:
    print "Invalid input. Please select a, b, c or d.
    /exit to exit"
```

15. Save the program as spaceShip.py in the Adventure 1 folder and run it using Run➪Run Module.

Figure 1-16 shows the full program. Once the program is running you can give it some commands. Try flying to a new planet or firing the cannons. What happens if you don't use one of the main commands?

FIGURE 1-16 The finished program

ADVENTURES IN PYTHON

Python Command Quick Reference Table

Command	Description
print	The print statement is used to output values onto the Python shell. For example print "cats" would output the word cats.
"string"	Strings are the data type to use when you want to store text in your program. A string stores characters, letters and symbols.
raw_input("question")	Use the raw_input() function to input string from the users into a program.
"Hello " + "Dave"	Concatenation uses the plus sign (+) to combine two or more strings. It is particularly useful when combining strings with strings that are stored in variables.
name = "Ellen"	Variables store data, which can be reused and changed in the program. Strings can be stored in variables.
if condition == True:	An if statement is used to control whether or not a section of code runs. It uses a condition to decide whether or not the code it contains should run. If the condition evaluates to True, it will run; otherwise it will not.
==	The *equals to* comparator is used with if statements and while loops to check whether the value of two things are the same. If they are the same it will evaluate to True; otherwise it will evaluate to False.
if..else	An else statement is used with an if statement. It will run code in the body of the else statement if the condition of the if statement evaluates to False.
if..elif..else	An elif statement is used with an if statement. It has its own condition and will run if this condition evaluates to True and the condition of the accompanying if statement evaluates to False.
while	A while loop will repeat a block of code. Like an if statement, it has a condition and will only repeat while its condition is True. If the condition is False it will not repeat.
!=	The *not equals to* comparator will check whether two values are not equal to each other. If they are equal it will evaluate to False, otherwise it will evaluate to True.
\n	The \n escape sequence is used in strings to create a new line.
import time	The import statement allows your program to use other pre-written modules with extra functions. The time module is one such module. It allows your programs to use timing instructions, such as waiting a few seconds.
time.sleep(5)	The sleep() function makes the program wait and do nothing for a number of seconds. The number of seconds is given as an argument inside the brackets. It can only be used if the time module has been imported.

Achievement Unlocked: Accomplished the creation of basic Python programs with input and output.

Next Adventure

So far you have learned about sequencing, outputting data, strings, concatenation, input, `if` statements, `else` statements, `elif` statements and `while` loops. You're doing really well! You will revisit all of these concepts in later adventures, and built upon them. Next up is Adventure 2, in which you'll use Python to create art… using a turtle!

Adventure 2

Drawing with Turtle Graphics

WITH PROGRAMMING IN Python, you can create a huge range of things, from games to scientific data analysis programs, and from 3D modelling tools to robot controllers. In Adventure 1, you learned how to use some basic Python code to make a spaceship command console. Now you're going to try something a bit more visual.

Creating images with Python is a fun and powerful way to learn how to program. What's great about it is that you can create complex images with programs that use only a few lines of Python code.

In this adventure, you'll learn how to use numbers and Turtle Graphics to make drawings with Python. Figure 2-1 shows a drawing made with Turtle Graphics.

Getting Started with Turtle

For a video that walks you through the steps of getting started with the `turtle` module, visit the companion website at www.wiley.com/go/adventuresinpython. Click the Videos tab and select the appropriate file.

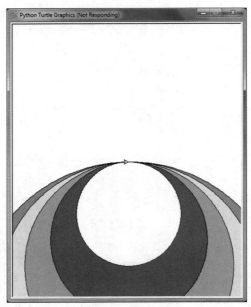

FIGURE 2-1 An example of a drawing made with Turtle Graphics.

In this adventure, you'll use the `turtle` module in Python. A **module** is a set of pre-written and reusable commands that extend what you can do with Python. Recall that you used the `time` module in Adventure 1 to make your program wait a number of seconds before proceeding. The `turtle` module allows you to create basic shapes and drawings in Python.

A **module** is a pre-written set of functions that can be imported into your Python programs. They allow your programs to do things that would not normally be possible without the module.

When you draw in Turtle Graphics, the cursor on your screen is referred to as a *turtle*, even though the default icon for the cursor doesn't look like a turtle! It actually looks like an arrow—but it is still called a turtle. You can imagine a turtle walking across your screen, leaving a trail behind it to create shapes and images. You'll most often use the `turtle` module simply to draw lines. By creating lots of lines, turning the turtle round, changing colours and filling in shapes, you'll discover that you can generate some really cool and complex images using only a few lines of Python.

Time to get started.

1. Open a Python shell by opening IDLE. (Remember that you can tell you are using the shell, rather than a text editor, as the shell has a command prompt (>>>) at the start of the line.)

2. To use the `turtle` module in your program, the first thing you need to do is import it. Type the following command into the shell to import the `turtle` module:

```
import turtle
```

3. Next, you're going to move the turtle (cursor) forward. To do this, you use the `turtle.forward()` command and include an argument to tell it how many steps to take. In this example, you'll start by moving the turtle 100 steps. When you put the 100 in between the brackets, you do not need to use speech marks as you're using numbers, not strings (more on this in a bit):

```
turtle.forward(100)
```

4. Press Enter. A new window will appear and a small arrow will move across the window, leaving a line behind it. This arrow is the "turtle," and it's just drawn a line 100 steps long, as shown in Figure 2-2.

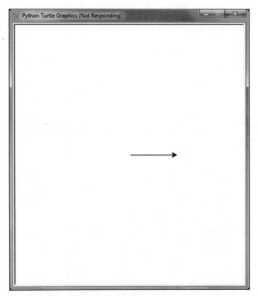

FIGURE 2-2 The turtle after moving 100 steps

5. You can continue to give the turtle commands from the shell. Type in the following code on the next line:

```
turtle.right(90)
```

Press Enter, and the turtle turns 90 degrees to the right.

6. Now enter the following commands into the shell one at a time, pressing Enter at the end of each line:

```
turtle.forward(50)
turtle.right(90)
turtle.forward(100)
turtle.right(90)
turtle.forward(50)
turtle.right(90)
```

Et voila! The turtle will have drawn a rectangle. It should now be back where it started, as shown in Figure 2-3.

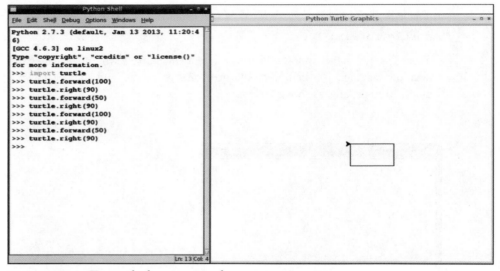

FIGURE 2-3 The turtle drew a rectangle.

You can of course change the arguments that you give the `right()` and `forward()` functions.

You have used **integers** in this program. Integers are whole numbers (that is, numbers with no decimal place) and can be either positive or negative. For example, 10, 92, 3, -78 and -831,789 are all integers.

An **integer** is a data type that is used to store whole numbers. For example, 1, 26 and 6546 are all whole numbers as they do not have a decimal place.

A **data type** determines the values that can be used for variables and other things such as function arguments. For example, the string data type only allows you to use values that are in speech marks and the integer data type only allows you to use whole numbers.

CHALLENGE

Can you work out how to draw a square? Squares have four sides that are the same length and each angle is 90 degrees.

Using Variables to Change Angles and Lengths

For a video that walks you through the steps of using variables to change angles and lengths, visit the companion website at www.wiley.com/go/adventuresinpython. Click the Videos tab and select the appropriate file.

The values used for arguments in the turtle functions can be swapped for variables. This next program uses variables for two things: the length of the sides; and the angles. The turtle will draw a zigzag line in this program. You'll also notice a new command, `left()`, which, as you might have guessed, makes the turtle turn left.

1. Open a new file editor by going to File⇨New Window.

2. As you know, whenever you use a module you need to import it. Add this line of code to import the `turtle` module:

```
import turtle
```

3. Create a variable called `length` and another called `angle` and set their values to 20 and 45, respectively:

```
length = 20
angle = 45
```

4. You want the turtle to move and turn to create a zigzag. Type this code:

```
turtle.forward(length)
turtle.right(angle)
turtle.forward(length)
turtle.left(angle)
```

5. Highlight the four lines of code that you just wrote, copy it and paste them in your file at least four times.

6. Run the program with Run⇨Run Module. Create a folder named `Adventure 2` and save the file in it as `zigZag.py`. Now when you run the program it will draw a zigzag as in Figure 2-4, making each length 20 steps and each angle 45 degrees.

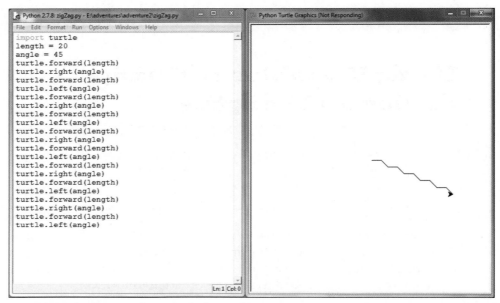

FIGURE 2-4 A zigzag drawn with the turtle

 You can download the completed `zigZag.py` code file and other code in this chapter from the companion website at www.wiley.com/go/adventuresinpython but you will learn more by typing in the code as you work through the steps.

One of the most useful features of variables is that you can change the value that they store. Here's an example for you to try, which should demonstrate the power of variables.

1. Open the program you just wrote (the one you saved as `zigZag.py`).

2. Change the `angle` variable so that it has the value of 90, instead of 45:

```
angle = 90
```

When you run the program you should see that the angle of each zigzag is now 90 degrees, as in Figure 2-5. This is because the value of the `angle` variable has been changed.

Change the value of the `length` variable and run the program to see how this affects the shape of the zigzag.

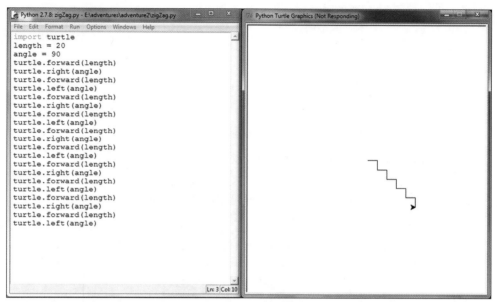

FIGURE 2-5 The updated code with a new value for the `angle` variable

CHALLENGE

Add extra lines of code to your program to change the variables for length and angle. Put these lines in between any of the other lines of code in your program. For example, you could change the first zigzag by changing the code to this:

```
turtle.forward(length)
turtle.right(angle)
length = 20
turtle.forward(length)
angle = 61
turtle.length(angle)
```

Run the code to see the result. Try experimenting with different values.

Using Addition to Draw a Spiral

As you have just seen, you can change the value of a variable to change the result of your program. But there's a lot more you can do—you can also change the value using addition, subtraction, multiplication and division. You're now going to use addition to draw a spiral with the turtle.

1. Create a new file editor in IDLE using File⇨New Window.

2. Import the `turtle` module and set the `length` and `angle` variables with the following code:

```
import turtle
length = 10
angle = 90
```

3. Now add this code to make the turtle move:

```
turtle.forward(length)
turtle.left(angle)
```

4. Next add the following code to make the length of the side increase by 10:

```
length = length + 10
```

5. Copy the last three lines of code and paste them at least 10 times, each set below the other. Now when you run the program, the length of the line will increase by 10 steps every time the turtle moves. The result? A spiral.

6. Save the program as `spiral.py` in the `Adventure 2` folder and run it with Run⇨Run Module. You should see a spiral like the one shown in Figure 2-6.

CRAIG SAYS... With Python you can use maths operations on values in your program. For example, you can use them to change the values of variables. You've already come across the addition operator (+); there are also operators for subtraction (-), multiplication (*) and division (/).

CHALLENGE

Change the angle to make the spiral decrease in size.

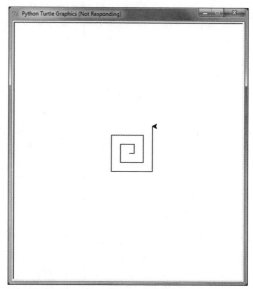

FIGURE 2-6 A spiral

Saving Some Space with Loops

For a video that walks you through the steps of saving space with loops, visit the companion website at www.wiley.com/go/adventuresinpython. Click the Videos tab and select the appropriate file.

It's not a good idea to copy and paste a block of code many times in a program. What happens if you want to change something? If you've pasted the code lines in 20 times, you would have to make 20 changes! You might be able to do it quickly if you've only got a few commands, but it soon gets very time consuming if there are lots of lines of code, and you may sometimes have hundreds or even thousands of lines. So much repeated code also makes the program harder to read and understand. There is a simpler way to it.

As you learned in Adventure 1, loops are an efficient way to repeat blocks of code. In this next example, you use a loop to create a spiral instead of copying and pasting the lines of code over and over again.

1. As before, create a new file editor in IDLE using File⇨New Window.

2. Import the turtle module and create length and angle variables:

```
import turtle
length = 0
angle = 90
```

3. Next, add a loop to make the steps repeat:

```
while length < 200:
    turtle.forward(length)
    turtle.right(angle)
    length = length + 10
```

4. Save the program as betterSpiral.py in the Adventure 2 folder.

5. Run the program with Run⇨Run Module. When the program starts, the turtle will start drawing a spiral, and you should end up with a new, improved spiral like the one in Figure 2-7.

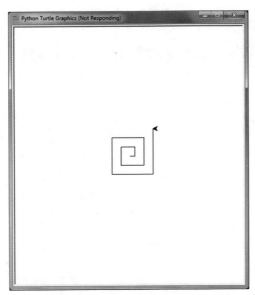

FIGURE 2-7 An even better spiral, made with a while loop

Notice how your program can draw a lot more than it did in the previous example, while using fewer lines of code.

The while loop in this code uses a *less than* **comparator**. It checks that the length of the line being drawn is less than 200. The body of the loop will repeat only when the length is less than 200. If it is equal to 200 or greater than 200, the loop will stop running. You can change this number to make a bigger or smaller spiral.

A **comparator** is used to compare two values. You have already used the *equal to* comparator, which compares two values to see if they are the same. The comparison will evaluate to either `True` of `False`, depending on whether or not the condition of the comparison is met.

There are six types of comparators that you can use in your own programs:

- Equal to (==): Checks whether two values are the same
- Not equal to (!=): Checks whether two values are not the same
- Less than (<): Compares a value to see if it less than another value
- Less than or equal to (<=): Compares a value to see if it is less than or the same as another value
- Greater than (>): Compares a value to see if it is greater than another value
- Greater than or equal to (>=): Compares a value to see if it is greater than or the same as another value

All of these comparators can be used with `if` statements and `while` loops.

A Shape with 360 Sides: Drawing a Circle

So far, the programs that you've written have only used straight lines. But what about circles? They don't use straight lines, just a single curved line. How can the turtle program create a curved line?

There's a simple solution to this: you create a curve simply by using lots and lots of very short straight lines with small turns. If your program creates 360 lines and 360 turns of 1 degree, it will result in a circle. Try it out for yourself:

1. Open a new file editor window in IDLE using File⇨New Window.

2. Save the file as `circle.py` in the `Adventure 2` folder.

3. Type the following code into the file editor:

```
import turtle
repeats = 0
while repeats < 360:
    turtle.forward(1)
    turtle.right(1)
    repeats = repeats + 1
```

4. Run the program using Run⇨Run Module. The turtle should draw a circle like the one shown in Figure 2-8.

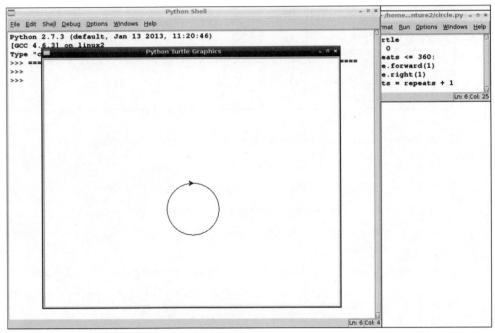

FIGURE 2-8 A circle drawn with the turtle

Controlling the Number of Sides Using for Loops

You can create quite an array of shapes by adapting the code from the example you just completed. You could change the program so that it creates a square or a triangle, for example. Can you work out how to do this? This next program uses input so that you can tell it how many sides you want your shape to have. The program uses a prompt that asks that very question.

DIGGING INTO THE CODE

The while loop and repeats variable are very important in this program. The first time the loop runs the value of the repeats variable is 0. The first line is drawn and the turtle turns by one degree. The value of the repeats variable is then increased by 1 and the loop starts again. This happens until the value of the repeats variable is 360. In other words, the program will draw a line for each of the 360 times the loop repeats. Although the loop doesn't repeat when the value of the variable is 360, it does repeat a total of 360 times. This is because when the repeats variable is 0 the code runs once, so 0 is counted as the first repeat of the loop.

1. Open IDLE and create a text editor using File➪New Window.

2. Save your program as `shapes.py` in the `Adventure 2` folder.

3. The next piece of code will produce a prompt asking you for input. The input value is used to determine how many sides your shape will have. Copy this code into the file editor:

```
import turtle
sides = int(raw_input("Enter the number of sides for ↵
                        your shape: "))
angle = 360.0 / sides
length = 400.0 / sides

for side in range(sides):
    turtle.forward(length)
    turtle.right(angle)
turtle.done()
```

The ↵ character at the end of a code line means that line and the next one should all be typed as a single line; do not add a line break or extra spaces between them.

CRAIG SAYS...

4. Run the program using Run➪Run Module. When you are prompted to enter the number of sides for your shape, type **7**. Figure 2-9 shows the result.

In this program, you have used a few things you haven't seen so far. Look at Step 3. On lines 3 and 4 the numbers have decimal places—in other words, they are not whole numbers, or integers but a different data type called a floating point number, or **float**. A float is the name for any number in Python that has a decimal place. Because floats and integers are both types of number, you can add, subtract, multiply and divide them.

On line 2 of the program, the `raw_input()` function is inside an `int()` function. The `raw_input()` function returns any data you input as a string—but your program needs to use your input as an integer, not a string. You therefore use the `int()` function to convert your input from a string to an integer. Converting one data type to another in this way is known as **type conversion**.

The code divides the total number of degrees in a circle (360) by the number that was input. This determines the degrees of each angle in the shape. The length of each side is determined by dividing 400 by the number that was input. These variables are then used to make the shape on the last four lines of the program.

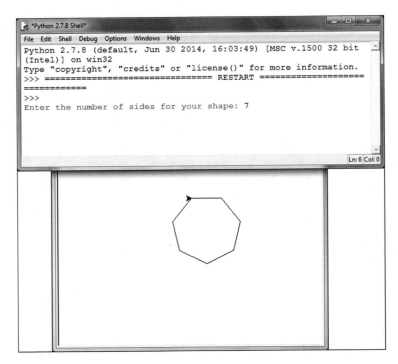

FIGURE 2-9 A seven-sided shape drawn with the `shapes.py` program

A **float** is a data type that stores numbers with decimal places. For example, 3.57, 668.1 and 45.5 are all examples of float values.

Type conversion is when one data type is changed into another data type. For example, a string that contains a number could be changed into an integer, or an integer could be changed into a string.

You have already come across one type of loop, the `while` loop. **For loops** are another type of loop that repeats a block of code. The `for` loop will repeat a number of times, determined by the argument inside the `range()` function. The `range()` function is very commonly used with `for` loops. You can also use `for` loops with lists, which you will learn about later. In the code you have just written, the loop will repeat the same number of times as is input for the number of sides. The argument of the `range()` function can be changed to another number to make the loop repeat a different number of times. For example, you could change the number of sides to four by using this code:

```
for sides in range(4):
    [etc…]
```

The last line of the program, `turtle.done()`, keeps the window open even after the shape has been drawn. Without it the program would close immediately after the shape has been drawn.

Changing the Fill Colour in a Shape

Now you've drawn a simple shape, what can you do to liven it up a bit? Add a bit of colour, that's what. With a simple change to the program, you can get your turtle to fill in the shape with colour. Here's how.

1. Open your `shapes.py` program, if it isn't open already.

2. On the line before the `for` loop, add the following lines of code:

```
turtle.fillcolor("blue")
turtle.begin_fill()
```

3. Next, on the second to last line of your program, add this line of code:

```
turtle.end_fill()
```

4. Save the program and run it with Run⇨Run Module. The turtle should draw a shape according to your input, but now the shape should be filled in with blue, as in Figure 2-10.

In the first Python statement you added, `turtle.fillcolor("blue")`, you selected the colour you wanted the turtle to use. There are a range of colours that you can use, including red, green, black and orange.

Try using different colours in your shapes; remember that they need to be written as a string. You will return to colours in a later adventure, when you learn more about using them, including how to create colours of your own.

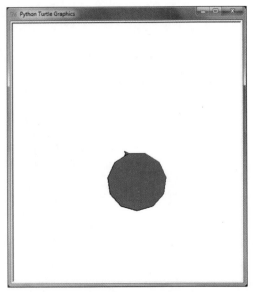

FIGURE 2-10 The turtle has drawn a shape with a fill colour of blue.

Creating Functions to Reuse Your Code

If you are starting to think like a computer programmer, you'll now be thinking: How can I save time? And how can I make more of my programs reusable? When you used the `raw_input()` function in Adventure 1, you learned that functions are one way that code can be made to be reusable. Now you're going to learn how to create your own functions to reuse code that draws shapes.

In the next example, you will use two functions to create shapes and move the position of the turtle.

1. Open a new file editor in IDLE using File⇨New Window.

2. Import the `turtle` module:

   ```
   import turtle
   ```

3. Now, add the following code to create a function that will draw a shape that can be any number of sides, with sides of any length, depending on the values you assign to the `sides` and `length` arguments. Type this code below the `import` command in the file editor:

   ```
   def drawShape(sides, length):
       angle = 360.0 / sides
       for side in range(sides):
           turtle.forward(length)
           turtle.right(angle)
   ```

4. Next add the following bit of code to let you move the turtle to a specific location on the screen:

```
def moveTurtle(x, y):
    turtle.penup()
    turtle.goto(x, y)
    turtle.pendown()
```

5. Now that you have created the two reusable functions, the program can call them to draw shapes and move the turtle. Add the following code to your program:

```
drawShape(4, 10)
moveTurtle(60, 30)
drawShape(3, 20)
turtle.done()
```

6. Save the program as reusableShapes.py in the Adventure 2 folder and run the program with Run⇨Run Module. You can see the output in Figure 2-11.

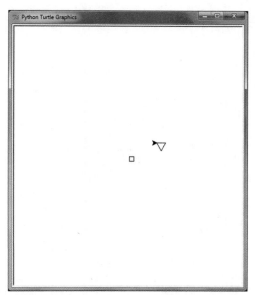

FIGURE 2-11 The program has drawn a couple of shapes.

You can now draw more shapes by calling the functions as many times as you want, using whatever arguments you like. This code uses the functions you just made to draw a shape with five sides and another shape with 10 sides. Add this code above the turtle.done() line:

```
moveTurtle(-100, -60)
drawShape(5, 100)
drawShape(10,100)
```

Arguments for `moveTurtle()` can be positive or negative numbers. What happens if you use negative numbers for the `drawShape()` function?

DIGGING INTO THE CODE

In the program you just wrote, in Step 3 you wrote a piece of code that creates a function called `drawShape()`. Remember that a function is a reusable set of instructions—lines of code that you can reuse again and again without having to type them out every time. You should be starting to get used to using pre-written functions like `raw_input()`, `turtle.forward()` and `int()`. For the first time, however, in the code you have just written, you have written your own function, `drawShape()`.

The `def` keyword at the start of the line in Step 3 states that you are creating (defining) a function. By giving the function a name, `drawShape()`, you made sure you can call it later.

Inside the brackets of the function, you have created two arguments, `sides` and `length`. This means that when your program calls this function you will give it two values that will affect how the function runs. `Sides` will determine how many sides the shape will have and `length` will determine the length of each side.

Notice that all of the statements inside of the function are indented by four spaces so that Python can identify that they belong to the function. The code in Step 4 creates a function named `moveTurtle`. It takes two arguments, `x` and `y`, and then moves the turtle to that location. The x and y variables represent coordinates on the drawing canvas, similar to points on a map. Coordinates are a way of describing a location using numbers: 0, 0 is the centre of the canvas for the turtle. The x coordinate determines how far up or down the turtle is and the y coordinate is how far to the left or right of centre the turtle is.

The `penup()` function in Step 4 makes the turtle stop drawing, as if the artist has lifted her pen off the paper. This means it can be moved without leaving a line behind it. The `pendown()` function makes the turtle start drawing again.

In order to use a function, you need to call it. Functions are reusable blocks of code, but by themselves they won't run unless called. Calling a function is basically telling the program that you want to use the function at that point in the program. You've called functions several times already, for example, when you used `raw_input()` or `str()`, these are both function calls. To call a function you just write its name, put brackets on the end and put any arguments inside the brackets.

When the functions are called they are passed the values for the variables in the same order that they are defined when the function is created. For example, drawShape() has two arguments, sides and length. In the final block of this code (in Step 5), when the function is called it is given the value 4 for sides and the value 10 for length. The next time the function is called it is given the value 3 for sides and 20 for length.

Shape Presets

Shapes with a predetermined number of sides, like triangles, circles, squares and pentagons, are very common. Instead of having to recreate the shape every time with the drawShape() function, wouldn't it be cool to add some code so that the common shapes have their own functions? For example, you could create a drawSquare() function that would instantly draw a square. Here's how:

1. Open the reusableShapes.py program that you just created. Underneath the moveTurtle() function add the following code:

```
def drawSquare(length):
    drawShape(4, length)
```

2. This code creates a new function to draw a square automatically. It reuses the drawShape() function and gives the drawShape() function the value of 4 for the sides argument. By doing this, the functions are reused so that your program uses fewer lines of code and is easier to read.

3. Add the following code to create functions for drawing triangles and circles:

```
def drawTriangle(length):
    drawShape(3, length)


def drawCircle(length):
    drawShape(360, length)
```

4. Now that you have created the functions to draw the shapes, the program can call them. To call all the shapes for which you have created a function, add the following code before the turtle.done() line in your program:

```
moveTurtle(-100, 20)
drawSquare(30)
moveTurtle(- 10, 20)
drawCircle(1)
drawCircle(2)
moveTurtle(75, -75)
drawTriangle(60)
```

5. Save the program and run it using Run⇨Run Module. The results should look something like Figure 2-12.

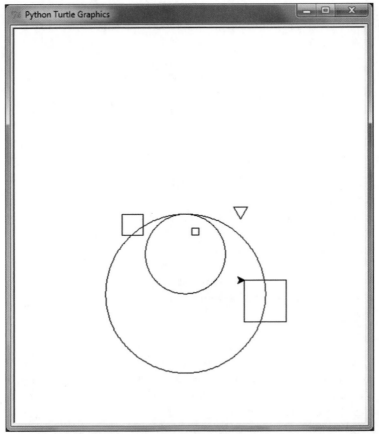

FIGURE 2-12 Shapes created using the functions and the example code

Adding Randomly Generated Pictures

Now that your program can reuse functions to create images, this is where things get interesting! You can easily change the code to draw some cool things. You can use the functions to quickly draw complex shapes with only a few lines of Python, or draw pictures by combining the different functions.

The next thing you're going to do is make your turtle draw completely random shapes all over the screen, a bit like in Figure 2-13.

FIGURE 2-13 A randomly generated picture

1. Open the `reusableShapes.py` program and save it as `randomShapes.py` in the `Adventure 2` folder.

2. Delete all the lines that contain function calls. Once you've done that, the only thing left in the program will be the following Python code:

```python
import turtle

def drawShape(sides, length):
    angle = 360.0 / sides
    for side in range(sides):
        turtle.forward(length)
        turtle.right(angle)
```

```
def moveTurtle(x, y):
    turtle.penup()
    turtle.goto(x, y)
    turtle.pendown()

def drawSquare(length):
    drawShape(4, length)

def drawTriangle(length):
    drawShape(3, length)

def drawCircle(length):
    drawShape(360, length)
```

In other words, what's left are all the functions that you created in the program.

3. Next, add this line of code at the very start of the program to import a new module, random:

```
import random
```

Add the following function to create a random shape at a random location:

```
def drawRandom():
    x = random.randrange(-;200, 200)
    y = random.randrange(-;200, 200)
    length = random.randrange(75)
    shape = random.randrange(1, 4)

    moveTurtle(x, y)

    if shape == 1:
        drawSquare(length)
    elif shape == 2:
        drawTriangle(length)
    elif shape == 3:
        length = length % 4
        drawCircle(length)
```

4. Finally, at the end of your program, add this loop to generate 100 random shapes and add the turtle.done() function:

```
for shape in range(100):
    drawRandom()
turtle.done()
```

5. Now save the program and run it using Run⇨Run Module. Your turtle will set off as if it has a mind of its own, drawing random shapes in random locations on the screen.

DIGGING INTO THE CODE

This function uses the `random` module to randomly generate values for the location and size of each shape that it creates. It also uses the module to generate a number, which is then used by the `if` statement to select which shape it will draw. You use the `randrange()` function from the `random` module to generate a random integer. It can take one or two arguments; when you give it one argument it will generate a number between 0 and the value of the argument given. For example, `random.randrange(60)` will generate a number between 0 and 60. When you give it two arguments, it will generate a number between the two numbers.

The `if` statement in the function chooses which shape to draw. The `shape` variable contains a randomly generated number between 1 and 3, which determines which shape is drawn.

The `%` on the line above the `drawCircle()` function call is called a **modulo** operation. This is like division except that instead of returning how many times one number will divide by another it works out the remainder of the division. For example, 7 divided by 3 is 2 with a remainder of 1 that cannot be divided, to leave an integer. The modulo operator is used in this program to make sure that the size of the circle isn't too big.

A **modulo** operation (%) is like the division operator, but instead of evaluating to the value of one number divided by another, it evaluates to the value of the remainder of the division. For example, 7 % 3 is 1 as 7 / 3 is 2 remainder 1.

For further adventures with Turtle Graphics, use the commands in the following quick reference table to experiment.

Python Command Quick Reference Table	
Command	**Description**
`import turtle`	This statement imports the `turtle` module and allows the program to create drawings using Turtle Graphics.
`turtle.forward(10)`	This command moves the turtle forward a number of steps and makes it draw a straight line.
`turtle.right(45)`	This command turns the turtle a number of degrees to the right.

continued

Python Command Quick Reference Table continued

Command	Description
`turtle.left(90)`	This command turns the turtle a number of degrees to the left.
`5` (Integers)	Whole numbers in Python use the integer data type; 5, 237 and 21 are all examples of integers.
`cats = 9`	Integers can be stored in variables. This allows the value of the variable to be reused and changed as the program runs.
`+` (addition)	The addition operator is used to add two number values together. The result is usually stored in a variable like this: `cats = 9 + 1`.
`<` (less than)	The `<` comparator compares two values. If the first value is less than the second, it evaluates to `True`, otherwise it evaluates to `False`.
`<=` (less than or equal to)	The `<=` comparator compares two values. If the first value is less than or the same as the second, it evaluates to `True`, otherwise it evaluates to `False`.
`int()`	The `int()` function converts values of other data types into the integer data type. It is most commonly used to turn strings into numbers.
`5.6` (floats)	Floats are a data type used to represent numbers with decimal places; 6.8, 11.51 and 574.96 are all examples of floats.
`/` (division)	The division operator divides one number by another. The result is often stored in a variable like so: `cake = 10 / 5`. Dividing an integer by another integer will evaluate to an integer, however dividing an integer by a float will evaluate to a float.
`for..in`	A `for` loop will repeat a block of code a number of times.
`turtle.fillcolor("red")` `turtle.begin_fill()` ... `turtle.end_fill()`	These functions are used in the `turtle` module to set the fill colour of the shapes being drawn by the turtle.
`def` (functions)	Functions are created using the `def` keyword. Once created, they can be called from anywhere in the program.
`%` (modulo)	The modulo operator divides one number by the other and returns the remainder of the division. For example, `7 % 3` would evaluate to `1` (7 divides by 3, 2 times, with 1 left over).
`import random`	The `random` module contains functions that randomly generate numbers.
`random.randrange()`	The `randrange()` function generates a random integer. The arguments of the function set the minimum and maximum numbers for the random number.

Achievement Unlocked: **Creator of splendid shapes using the** `turtle` **module.**

Next Adventure

Now you know how to draw shapes with Python's `turtle` module. You've also started using integers, maths operations, `for` loops and floats. Oh—and you've created your own functions. Wow, that's quite a lot! But there's more to come.

In the next adventure, you'll learn how to create windows and buttons with Python. You'll create a random sentence generator and a whole lot of other cool programs.

Adventure 3
Windows, Buttons, and Other GUI Stuff

WHEN YOU USE computers, you're probably used to interacting with programs using both a mouse and a keyboard. You click buttons and things happen. You enter information into text boxes, read messages displayed in dialogue boxes, and resize, minimise and close the boxes in which you've been working.

So far on your adventures here, you have created programs that interact with the user only by using text—in other words, you have only made programs that use **Commandline Interfaces** (or **CLI**). CLIs only allow users to interact with them through commands given from the keyboard and don't allow them to use a mouse. You have been creating these programs by using the `raw_input()` function, where a prompt appears in the command line so the user can enter some characters that are then passed to the program. These programs are straightforward for programmers like yourself, of course! But most people expect programs to be nicely packaged in a window with buttons and all the other stuff they're used to.

In this adventure, you'll learn how to provide users with all of that, by creating **Graphical User Interfaces** (or **GUI**, which some people pronounce as "gooey"). A GUI is a program that allows the person using it to interact with it using a mouse and keyboard. Figure 3-1 shows a simple example of a GUI.

FIGURE 3-1 A simple GUI made in `Tkinter`

Commandline Interfaces (CLI) are user interfaces that allow interaction only through text-based commands. They do not respond to mouse input.

Graphical User Interfaces (GUI) are user interfaces that use windows, icons and buttons to interact with the user. GUIs allow the use of mice and keyboards.

In this adventure, you will become familiar with a module called `Tkinter`, which you use with Python to create GUIs. You'll create some short programs that use buttons, text boxes and labels and then create a program that uses a button to generate random sentences. Let's get going!

Creating Buttons

For a video that walks you through the steps of creating buttons, visit the companion website at www.wiley.com/go/adventuresinpython. Click the Videos tab and select the appropriate file.

In the first part of this adventure, you will create a basic program that creates a button. As the adventure progresses, you'll make the button do different things when you click it. To start off, you'll use the following code to create a button that will print `Beep!` to the Python shell when you click it.

1. Open IDLE and create a new window using File⇨New Window.

2. Create a new folder called `Adventure 3` and save the new file as `button.py`.

3. Before you do anything else, you need to enable your Python program to use the `Tkinter` module. Type the following code into your file:

```
import Tkinter as tk
window = tk.Tk()
```

The first line imports the functions from the `Tkinter` library and renames it to `tk` so that it is easier to spell. The second line then creates a `Tkinter` window so that it can now be used by Python.

4. Next, add some code to tell the button what to do when you click it:

```
def buttonClick():
    print "Beep!"
```

The `buttonClick()` function is used with the button. Later in the program this function will be called when the button is pressed, but it is not linked up just yet. In this case the program will print `Beep!` to the Python shell. You've called the function `buttonClick()`, but you can actually call the function anything you like, as long as it matches the argument you give to the button later in the program.

5. Now you need some code to create the button and place it on the window:

```
button = tk.Button(window, text="Click me!",
    command=buttonClick)
button.pack()
window.mainloop()
```

The line with the `button` variable creates a new button using the `tk.Button()` function. The first argument, `window`, states where the button will be placed; in this case it will be placed on the window that was created at the start of the program. The `text= "Click me!"` argument tells the function what to display on the button. This is an example of a named argument; you can read about these in the Digging Into the Code sidebar that follows.

Finally, the last argument states which function will be run when the button is clicked. In this case, the program will run the `buttonClick()` function created earlier in the program.

The `pack()` function works out the size and position of the button and then actually displays the button on the window. The `pack()` function knows to put the button on the window as this was given as the first argument when the button was created. Without the `pack()` function, the button would not be displayed. The `mainloop()` function is run at the end of all `Tkinter` programs. It makes the window appear and handles all the button presses and other stuff when the program is running.

6. Save the program again and click Run⇨Run Module.

7. After a short pause, a window should appear with a button displaying the words `Click me!` (see Figure 3-2). Click the button and `Beep!` will be printed to the Python shell.

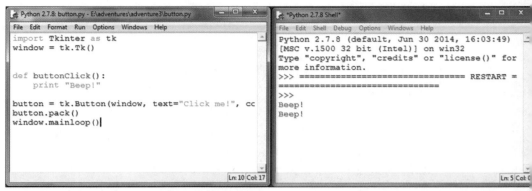

FIGURE 3-2 The window with a button and the output from the click shown in the Python shell.

CRAIG SAYS You can download the completed `button.py` code file and other code in this chapter from the companion website at www.wiley.com/go/adventuresinpython but you will learn more by typing in the code as you work through the steps.

DIGGING INTO THE CODE

Named arguments (also called keyword arguments) are a way of explicitly stating to the function what you want the values of different arguments to be. For example, in the program above the code `text="Click me!"` tells the function that you want the value of the text argument to be `"Click me!"`. Why would you choose to do this? Up until now you've given functions arguments in the order that they are when the function is defined. However, for functions that have a lot of arguments or don't require every argument to have a value, it is easier to use named arguments. Named arguments can be used in any order in the function call.

The `Tkinter` button is a type of `Tkinter` **widget**. A widget is a reusable piece of code that creates an element on the GUI. For example, a button, a slider and a text box are all examples of `Tkinter` widgets. Widgets are very useful because how they behave is already written, and they are reusable. For example, when you click a button the widget's pre-written code tells it what to look like and how to behave. This saves a lot of time and effort as you as a programmer can reuse this code without needing to write it all from scratch.

Changing the Button Text on Click

By changing the code in the `buttonClick()` function, you can make clicking the button result in a different outcome.

This function isn't just fun, it is also great for testing to see how the button works. But it's not a good idea to print things to the Python shell for a finished program when you're using a GUI. Instead, the program should aim to display all of the output in the GUI and not the shell. This is because it's not very intuitive for someone using your program to interact with one window (for example, clicking a button) and have information appear in another. It is more intuitive when information is displayed in the window that the user interacts with.

What if you want the text on the button itself to change when you click it? With `Tkinter` you can change the text on buttons after the program has started running. Follow these steps to change the text on the button from `Click me!` to `Clicked` after it is clicked:

1. Change the `buttonClick()` function to this:

   ```
   def buttonClick():
       button.config(text="Clicked")
   ```

2. Save the program.

3. Run the program using Run➪Run Module.

4. Click the button and the text on it will change to say it has been clicked, as you can see in Figure 3-3.

You'll notice that this change to the program uses the `button.config()` function. This function allows **properties** stored about the button to be changed. For example, in your program the `text` property is changed to `Clicked` using this function. In the next section, you'll learn how to use `button.config()` to count how many times the button has been clicked!

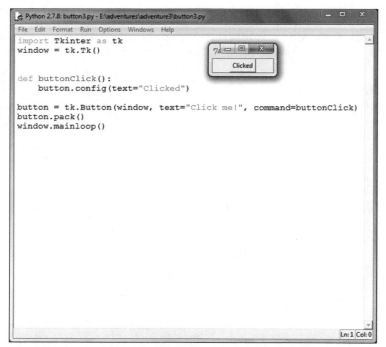

FIGURE 3-3 When the button is clicked, the text on the button changes.

A **property** is data stored about a widget in `Tkinter`. For example, the text on a button is stored as a property, so are its size, colour and a whole load of other things.

Counting Clicks

With a slight change to the `button.py` program, you can make it record the number of times the button has been clicked. Counting the number of times a button has been clicked is useful in a number of situations. For example, you could use the count to change the text on the button depending on the number of times it has been clicked. The next bit of code will show you how to do this.

1. Open your `button.py` program and save it as `buttonCount.py` in the `Adventure 3` folder.

2. Replace the `buttonClick()` function with the following code, making sure you include the first line outside the function that creates the `count` variable:

```
count = 0

def buttonClick():
    global count
    count = count + 1
    button.config(text=str(count))
```

3. Save the program.

4. Run it using Run➪Run Module.

When the window appears, click the button several times. Each time you click it, it will update to display the number of times you have clicked it (see Figure 3-4).

FIGURE 3-4 The button after it has been clicked seven times

DIGGING INTO THE CODE

This code works by using the `count` variable to record the number of times the button has been clicked. The `count` variable is created outside of the function so that it can store values even after the function has finished. The bit of code that says `global count` allows the function to change the value of `count`. Every time the function is called, the `count` variable has 1 added to it. The final line updates the text on the button to display the number of times it has been clicked.

The `str()` function is like the `int()` function, but it does the opposite. The `str()` function takes non-string data, such as integers and floats, and converts them into strings. This is useful as many functions expect strings as their arguments and using integers or floats instead of a string will cause an error.

Can you work out how to add two buttons in the same window? How would you change the counter when each button is clicked? Can you work out how to make a counter for each button? How would you update the text on each button separately?

Creating Text Boxes

VIDEO

For a video that walks you through the steps of creating text boxes, visit the companion website at www.wiley.com/go/adventuresinpython. Click the Videos tab and select the appropriate file.

As mentioned earlier in this adventure, it is not a good idea to display information in the Python shell when using a GUI. Neither is it a good idea to collect user input from the Python shell. Instead, you should aim to contain all input and output in the GUI.

You learned in previous adventures how to input data using the `raw_input()` function in Python. This function is quite straightforward to use, but it means the user has to type the input into the shell, so it is not very practical when you are creating a GUI. It is important to keep all the data input on the GUI in order to make your program usable for new users, so in this case the `raw_input()` function is not a good choice.

The `entry` widget in `Tkinter` allows you to create text entry boxes on your GUIs. These are easy to use, and you can set them up with just a few lines of Python code.

Your next program will create a GUI with a text entry box and a button. When the window appears it will have a button and a text box. Every time the button is pressed it will copy and paste the text, so that it appears twice. Follow these steps to create the program:

1. Open IDLE and open the file editor using File⇨New Window.

2. Save the file as `double.py` in the `Adventure 3` folder.

3. Type the following two lines at the start of the program. As you've done before, this piece of code will import the instructions from `Tkinter` and allow your program to use these instructions:

```
import Tkinter as tk
window = tk.Tk()
```

4. Next create the `changeString()` function by typing this code into your program:

```
def changeString():
    stringToCopy = entry.get()
    entry.insert(0, stringToCopy)
```

The `changeString()` function will be called when a button is clicked. The first line gets the contents of a text entry box and stores it in the `stringToCopy` variable. The second line inserts the string back into the entry text box at position 0. In short, this duplicates the contents of the text box. Note that the `entry` widget is not created until later in the program.

5. Next type these lines of code to create a text entry field and a button:

```
entry = tk.Entry(window)
button = tk.Button(window, text="Change", command=change
    String)
```

The `entry` variable stores a `Tkinter` button. It is placed on top of the window that was initialised earlier in the program. A button is created, the same as before, and calls the `changeString()` function when clicked.

6. Finally, type these last three lines of code. They place the text entry field and button onto the window, then make the window open and manage all events that happen inside it:

```
entry.pack()
button.pack()
window.mainloop()
```

7. Save the program and click Run⇨Run Module.

8. When the `Tkinter` window opens, enter some text in the text box and then click the button. You will see the text duplicate itself. The text will double every time you click the button, as you can see in Figure 3-5.

The first argument in the `entry.insert()` function is 0. What happens if you change this integer to another number, like 4?

CHALLENGE

Can you work out how to add the string `"Hello,"` to the text box contents, instead of duplicating the text, whenever the button is pressed?

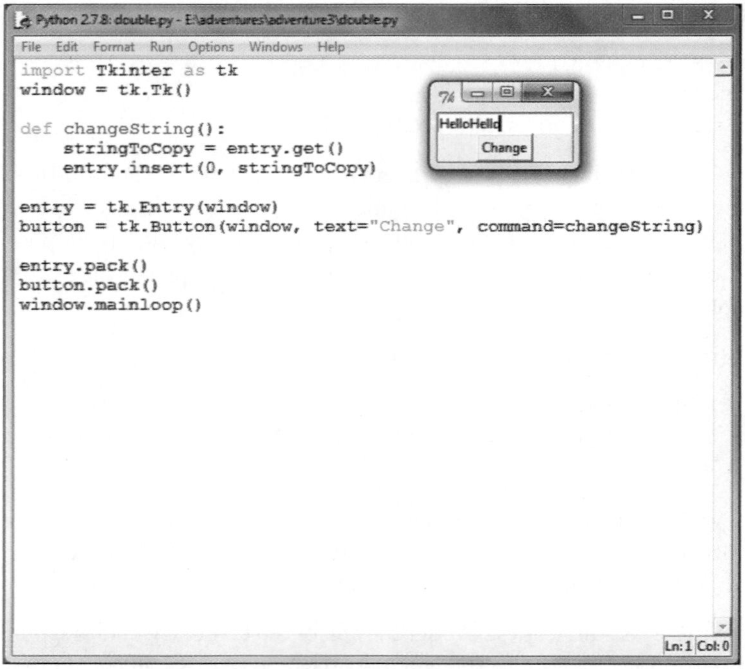

FIGURE 3-5 The text box after the button has been pressed

Writing It Backwards

Let's have some fun and make the text appear backwards. You only need to make a small modification to the double.py program to do this:

1. Make sure the double.py program is open and save it as backwards.py in the Adventure 3 folder.

2. Change the changeString() function so that it contains the following lines of code:

```
def changeString():
    stringToCopy = entry.get()
    stringToCopy = stringToCopy[::-1]
    entry.delete(0, tk.END)
    entry.insert(0, stringToCopy)
```

3. Run the program by clicking Run⇨Run Module.

4. When the window pops up, enter some text in the text entry field. Click the button and the text will be reversed, as shown in Figure 3-6. Click it again and the text will return to normal.

```
Python 2.7.8: backwards.py - E:\adventures\adventure3\backwards.py
File  Edit  Format  Run  Options  Windows  Help
import Tkinter as tk
window = tk.Tk()


def changeString():
    stringToCopy = entry.get()
    stringToCopy = stringToCopy[::-1]
    entry.delete(0, tk.END)
    entry.insert(0, stringToCopy)

entry = tk.Entry(window)
button = tk.Button(window, text="Change", command=changeString)

entry.pack()
button.pack()
window.mainloop()



                                                          Ln: 1  Col: 0
```

FIGURE 3-6 The text box, reversed

Adding Passwords

Passwords are used to restrict access to information or certain features of a program. The text boxes that are used to input passwords usually don't show the password as it's being typed, but show an asterisk (*) in place of each character instead. That way, other people can't see the password.

You might be surprised to hear that it's really easy to make password boxes with Python and `Tkinter`. All you need to do is add an extra named argument, and the text entry field is turned into a password box.

You are now going to create a program that checks whether a password is correct. In the GUI there will be a field for entering the password and a button to submit the password. If the password is correct, a label will appear at the bottom with the text `Correct`, otherwise it will say `Incorrect`.

DIGGING INTO THE CODE

The password variable stores the correct password for the system. At the moment the password is Oranges, but feel free to change it to whatever you want. The enteredPassword variable gets the contents of the password entry box, and the if statement checks whether this matches the correct password. If the two passwords match, then the text in the Label widget is changed to Correct; otherwise it is changed to Incorrect. You haven't come across labels yet, but you're about to! They are simply uneditable text boxes in the GUI that are used to label things.

1. Open IDLE and create a new file editor window with File↪New Window.

2. Save the program as password.py in the Adventure 3 folder.

3. Type the first two lines of Python code into the file editor to import and initialise the program:

```python
import Tkinter as tk
window = tk.Tk()
```

4. Next create the checkPassword() function. As you can guess, this will check if the password entered is correct:

```python
def checkPassword():
    password = "Oranges"
    enteredPassword = passwordEntry.get()
    if password == enteredPassword:
        confirmLabel.config(text="Correct")
    else:
        confirmLabel.config(text="Incorrect")
```

5. Next, add the following code to create the password label and the password entry box:

```python
passwordLabel = tk.Label(window, text="Password:")
passwordEntry = tk.Entry(window, show="*")
```

6. Add this next bit of code into the file editor:

```python
button = tk.Button(window, text="Enter", command=check
  Password)
confirmLabel = tk.Label(window)
```

7. The next bit of code lays out all of the Tkinter widgets in the GUI. This label will be used to tell the users whether or not they have entered the correct password. The label is left blank when it is first created and is updated when the checkPassword() function is called. This final section of code adds all of the Tkinter widgets to the GUI and starts the GUI. Type it into the file editor:

```
passwordLabel.pack()
passwordEntry.pack()
button.pack()
confirmLabel.pack()

window.mainloop()
```

8. That's it! Save the program and run it using Run⇨Run Module. When the window appears, type in a random word and click the Enter button. You should see the label at the bottom of the window change to `Incorrect`. Try out some other words, and you should get the same result. Now enter the correct password. The default password for this program is `Oranges` (though you may have changed it). When you click the button with the correct password, the label at the bottom of the window should change to `Correct`, as in Figure 3-7.

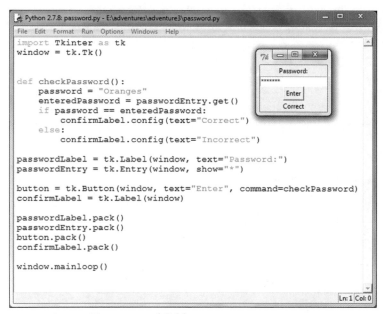

FIGURE 3-7 The password field

DIGGING INTO THE CODE

Labels in `Tkinter` are just a way of displaying strings on your GUI. They are simply text boxes in the GUI that are used to label things. You can't edit them by clicking on them, though the text in the label can be set and changed with Python code. The named argument `show` in the `Entry()` function makes each of the characters entered in the box show up as an asterisk (*) so no one can see what the user is typing. The characters are still entered normally, you just can't see what they are. You could change the character in the `show` argument from an asterisk to whatever you want, though if you choose a letter, it may be confusing for the user.

Building a Random Sentence Generator

VIDEO

For a video that walks you through the steps of creating a random generator, visit the companion website at www.wiley.com/go/adventuresinpython. Click the Videos tab and select the appropriate file.

You've already covered a lot of ground in this adventure and have learned how to create buttons and make things happen when you click them. Now you'll use those new skills to create an awesome program that generates random sentences.

This program is great fun. It takes a person's name and then chooses a verb and a noun to create a sentence. For example, if you enter the name Barry, it might generate a sentence like "Barry likes cakes" or, less believably, "Barry eats cats".

Lists are extremely useful in Python, as you're about to find out. In the random sentence generator program, you store any number of words in a list that will be used to randomly generate the sentences. There are only a small number of words stored in the sample program, so try adding your own to make the sentences even more random.

1. Open IDLE and create a new file editor using File⇨New Window.

2. Save the file as randomSentences.py in the Adventure 3 folder.

3. Type the following lines into the file editor. These import Tkinter and start it up, and also import the random module so that it can select random words from the supplied list.

```
import Tkinter as tk
import random
window = tk.Tk()
```

4. Below this, add the next bit of code, which will select a random word from your list of nouns:

```
def randomNoun():
    nouns = ["cats", "hippos", "cakes"]
    noun = random.choice(nouns)
    return noun
```

5. Add the next bit of code, which will select a random verb:

```
def randomVerb():
    verbs = ["eats", "likes", "hates", "has"]
    verb = random.choice(verbs)
    return verb
```

This works exactly the same as the `randomNoun()` function—the only difference is the contents of the list. See the Digging into the Code sidebar for an explanation of how this function works.

At the moment, the only nouns your program has to choose from are cats, hippos and cakes! Try adding some of your own. To add more words to the lists of nouns and verbs, simply write each word as a string and use commas to separate them from each other.

6. The next function generates the random sentence and places it in the text box at the bottom of the window. Add this code to the bottom of the program:

```
def buttonClick():
    name = nameEntry.get()
    verb = randomVerb()
    noun = randomNoun()
    sentence = name + " " + verb + " " + noun
    result.delete(0, tk.END)
    result.insert(0, sentence)
```

7. Now that you have written the functions, you can add the widgets for the window. You do this the same way as you did earlier in this adventure. This code adds a label that says Name, a text box to enter a name, a button that will generate a random sentence when clicked, and a text box to store the random sentence. Type the code into your program:

```
nameLabel = tk.Label(window, text="Name:")
nameEntry = tk.Entry(window)
button = tk.Button(window, text="Generate",
    command=buttonClick)
result = tk.Entry(window)
```

8. Finally, the last bit of the program lays out the text boxes, button and label in the window and starts the main loop. Add this to your file editor:

```
nameLabel.pack()
nameEntry.pack()
button.pack()
result.pack()
window.mainloop()
```

9. Now click Run⇨Run program to run your program.

10. When the window appears, type a name into the text box labelled Name. Click the Generate button and a random sentence of three words will appear at the bottom. Figure 3-8 shows the program in action. Just think of the possibilities—it can provide you with hours of entertainment!

```
Python 2.7.8: randomSentences.py - E:\adventures\adventure3\randomSentences.py

File  Edit  Format  Run  Options  Windows  Help

import Tkinter as tk
import random
window = tk.Tk()

def randomNoun():
    nouns = ["cats", "hippos", "cakes"]
    noun = random.choice(nouns)
    return noun

def randomVerb():
    verbs = ["eats", "likes", "hates", "has"]
    verb = random.choice(verbs)
    return verb

def buttonClick():
    name = nameEntry.get()
    verb = randomVerb()
    noun = randomNoun()
    sentence = name + " " + verb + " " + noun
    result.delete(0, tk.END)
    result.insert(0, sentence)

nameLabel = tk.Label(window, text="Name:")
nameEntry = tk.Entry(window)

button = tk.Button(window, text="Generate", command=buttonClick)
result = tk.Entry(window)

nameLabel.pack()
nameEntry.pack()
button.pack()
result.pack()

window.mainloop()

                                                                    Ln: 1  Col: 0
```

FIGURE 3-8 The finished random sentence generator

DIGGING INTO THE CODE

You have just used Python code to create lists and work with them. In Python, lists store a number of values in one variable. The nouns variable is a list of items (in this case, cats, hippos and cakes). Think of it like a shopping list. On your shopping list, you can have lots of items, like eggs, cake, cheese, milk, bread, sugar, tea and so on. If you wrote each of these items on a separate piece of paper, you would find it difficult to manage all the pieces of paper. This gets even more difficult the more pieces of paper you have. What would happen if you wanted to change an item or find it really quickly? So instead of writing your shopping list in many different places, you write it on a single piece of paper, making it easier to manage. The same principle applies with lists in Python. Instead of using lots of different variables for similar things, they can be stored in a single list, making it easier to manage.

To create a list in Python, you use square brackets: []. Every item on the list goes inside the brackets. Each item is separated by commas. For example, you could create a list of colours using the following code:

```
colours = ["red", "green", "blue", "red", "orange"]
```

Each item in this list is a string and therefore has speech marks around it. You may have noticed that `"red"` appears in the list twice. This is fine, Python doesn't mind; it counts each instance of red as two separate items in the list.

Lists can also store values of different data types. You don't have to store data that is only strings, or only integers or only floats. You can mix and match the different types. For example, you could have a list that contains strings and integers (notice that the integers do not need speech marks):

```
things = ["cheese", 6, "spanner", "telephone", 63]
```

When selecting the items in a list, the position of the first item is not counted as 1 but 0. You won't be using this knowledge in this chapter, but it's a good idea to think about it now. If the first item in a list is stored in position 0, what do you think the position of the second item in the list is?

The `choice()` function in Step 4 selects a random item from a list and returns it. In this program, it is stored in the `noun` variable.

The last line in Step 4 returns the value of the `noun` variable to the place in the program that called the function. There are two types of functions: those that return a value and those that don't. Functions that return values can be used in place of a value, so their result can be used to set variables or as arguments in functions.

The first line of the `buttonClick()` function in Step 6 gets the name that was entered in the `nameEntry()` text box. The second and third lines use the functions you created earlier to generate a random verb and a random noun. These three variables are then concatenated (joined) and stored in the sentence variable. The last two lines clear the 'result' text box and insert the new sentence.

Programming a Guessing Game

For a video that walks you through the steps of creating this guessing game, visit the companion website at www.wiley.com/go/adventuresinpython. Click the Videos tab and select the appropriate file.

As the final stage of this adventure, you'll use the new coding skills you learned in this adventure to create a number guessing game.

The game—surprise!—allows you to guess a number. When you press the button it will generate a random number and compare it with your guess. If you guessed the correct number you score a point, otherwise your score remains the same.

1. Open IDLE and create a file editor using File⇨New Window.

2. In the file editor add this code:

```
import random
import Tkinter as tk
window = tk.Tk()

maxNo = 10
score = 0
rounds = 0
```

CRAIG SAYS...

This program uses the `random` module so that it can generate random numbers.

By default, the game will allow you to guess any number between 1 and 10, but you can change the maximum guess by changing the value of the `maxNo` variable. The `score` and `rounds` variables are created so that the program can keep track of the player's score and the number of times they've made a guess.

3. The next bit of the code will run when the button is clicked. It works out whether you have entered a valid number and then whether or not your guess was correct. Afterwards, it updates the labels and text boxes on the screen. Add it to your program now:

```
def buttonClick():
    global score
    global rounds
    try:
        guess = int(guessBox.get())
        if 0 < guess <= maxNo:
            result = random.randrange(1, maxNo + 1)
            if guess == result:
                score = score + 1
            rounds = rounds + 1
        else:
            result = "Entry not valid"
    except:
        result = "Entry not valid"
    resultLabel.config(text=result)
    scoreLabel.config(text=str(score) + "/" + str(rounds))
    guessBox.delete(0, tk.END)
```

Are you unsure what you've just told the program to do? Read the Digging into the Code sidebar at the end of the example to figure it out.

4. The next bit of the program creates the labels, text entry and button that are used in the GUI. Type this into your program:

```
guessLabel = tk.Label(window, text="Enter a number from 1
   to " + str(maxNo))
guessBox = tk.Entry(window)
resultLabel = tk.Label(window)
scoreLabel = tk.Label(window)
button = tk.Button(window, text="guess", command=buttonClick)
```

5. Finally, add these statements to your program. They add the widgets to the GUI and make the main loop run:

```
guessLabel.pack()
guessBox.pack()
resultLabel.pack()
scoreLabel.pack()
button.pack()

window.mainloop()
```

6. Save the program as guessingGame.py in the Adventure 3 folder and run the program. When the window appears, enter a number into the text box. Click the button to generate a random number and the program will check whether your guess was the same as the random number. Figure 3-9 shows the completed game.

FIGURE 3-9 The finished guessing game

DIGGING INTO THE CODE

Need a bit of help following the code in Step 3? The value of the text box is stored as a string. In order to check whether it is greater than 0 and less than or equal to the maximum guess, it needs to be changed to an integer. The `int()` function accomplishes this task. Unfortunately, if the user has entered a nonnumerical value or hasn't entered anything at all, an error will occur. In order to handle this possibility, you use a `try...except` statement. The `try...except` statement will run the code inside the body of the `try` statement. If an error occurs it will stop running this bit and go to the body of the `except` statement and run that code. In this code, the error could be caused by entering something that can't be converted into an integer for the guess or no guess at all. The body of the `except` statement will set the output for the result to `Entry not valid`, which is displayed to the user in the `resultLabel`.

The first `if` statement in the body of the `try` statement checks whether the guess is between 1 and the maximum guess. It can also be equal to the maximum guess (the code checks that the guess is greater than 0, therefore the guess must be at least 1). If the value doesn't meet these criteria, the program will set the result to `Entry not valid`. The other `if` statement checks whether the guess was equal to the random number; if it was, the program will add 1 to the score.

Try entering letters, numbers bigger than 10, numbers smaller than 1, and leaving the text box blank. What results do you get? What do you think will happen if you enter 0? Why is this? What about when you enter 10?

For further adventures with `Tkinter` and the GUI, try the commands listed in the following quick table.

Python Command Quick Reference Table	
Command	**Description**
`import Tkinter as tk`	Importing the `Tkinter` module allows your program to create GUIs. Using the `as` operator renames the module so that it's easier to remember in the program.
`tk.Button()`	With the `Tkinter` module you can create buttons.
`button.pack()`	The `pack()` function is used to layout a `Tkinter` widget, such as a button, in a window.
`mainloop()`	The `mainloop()` function is used to make the `Tkinter` window appear on the screen and manages what happens when things like buttons are clicked. Omitting this function would mean that the window does not appear.
`str()`	This function converts data types, such as integers and floats, into strings.

Command	Description
`tk.Entry()`	Use the `Entry()` function to create text entry boxes in `Tkinter`.
`entry.get()`	This function returns the value in a text box.
`entry.insert()`	This function inserts a value into a text box. The value you want to insert should be given as an argument to the function.
`entry.delete()`	This function deletes the contents of a text box.
`reverse="this" [::-1]`	Adding `[::-1]` at the end of a string, or the end of a variable that contains a string, will reverse the string.
`label.config()`	The `config()` function is used to change properties of labels, buttons, and so on. Properties include the text inside the button.
`tk.Label()`	Labels place text in the `Tkinter` window. They cannot be modified by the user and are used to label other things.
`random.choice()`	The `choice()` function from the random module chooses a random item from a list.
`list = ["red", "yellow", "green", "blue"]`	Lists are a collection of values. They can be stored together in a single variable. Lists are a very important construct in Python.

Achievement Unlocked: **You can create GUIs with the `Tkinter` module.**

Next Adventure

In this adventure you learned how to use `Tkinter`. You created buttons, labels, windows and text boxes. You also learned a bit about random numbers, lists and functions that return values in Python.

In the next adventure, you will find out more about the exciting things you can do using `Tkinter` and will create a colour picker and a click speed game. You'll learn a lot along the way, including how to use sliders in `Tkinter` and how colours work on computers.

Adventure 4
More GUI Elements with Tkinter

IN ADVENTURE 3 you began to create GUIs using the `Tkinter` module in Python. You created different programs that used buttons, text boxes and labels. That little bit of knowledge can take you a very long way. By mixing and matching those few basic elements, you can create almost anything you can think of.

In this adventure, you'll take your knowledge of `Tkinter` one step further. You're about to embark on a series of small adventures in which you'll learn how to create a colour mixer and a click speed game. You'll also be introduced to the concepts behind the programs and different ways to modify how your program works so that you can create your own ideas.

Time to start!

Creating Sliders

For a video that walks you through the steps of creating a slider, visit the companion website at www.wiley.com/go/adventuresinpython. Click the Videos tab and select the appropriate file.

In this program, you'll create a colour picker. Before you start, let's look at one of the things you'll be using in your program: a slider.

So far in your `Tkinter` Python programs you have used text boxes to input data into your programs. Although this is very flexible, there are many other ways to input data.

A **Graphical User Interface (GUI)** is a program that uses graphics and icons for interaction with the user. GUIs use buttons, text boxes, sliders and a range of other things.

Sliders are used to input numerical data into your program. Look at Figure 4-1 to see an example of a GUI with a slider. Sliders use a knob and a path and give a number depending how far the knob is along the path. The further the knob is along the path, the higher the number.

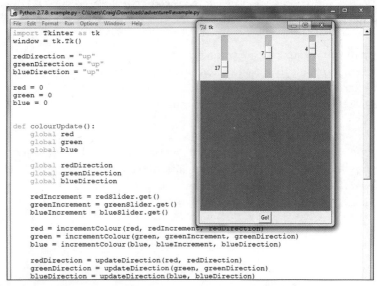

FIGURE 4-1 A GUI with a slider

In `Tkinter`, a slider is known as a `Scale`. Like other objects in `Tkinter` and Python, you can achieve a lot with only a few lines of code.

Time for you to create a super basic slider! The program you're about to create will simply create a `Tkinter` window with a slider—it won't do anything else but you'll build upon on this later. Look at Figure 4-2 to see what you will be creating.

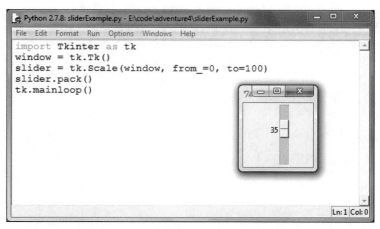

FIGURE 4-2 A Tkinter slider

1. Open IDLE and create a new file editor by clicking File ⇨ New Window.

2. Create a folder called `Adventure 4` and save the program in the folder as `slider.py`.

3. On the first line of the file editor add the following lines:

```
import Tkinter as tk
window = tk.Tk()
```

4. Next, you need to create a slider in your program. You achieve this with a single line:

```
slider = tk.Scale(window, from_=0, to=100)
```

5. Next you finish the program in the usual way, by packing the slider and running the main loop:

```
slider.pack()
tk.mainloop()
```

6. Save the program.

7. Run the program using Run ⇨ Run Module.

8. A small window with a slider should appear. Try sliding the slider by clicking the knob and dragging it up and down.

Look at that sliding action. Up, down, in the middle, just above the middle. Notice how the numbers update as you move the slider. Neat, isn't it?

DIGGING INTO THE CODE

As with all other `Tkinter` programs, the first line of code imports the `Tkinter` Python functions into your program so that it can use them. The second line then creates a new instance of `Tkinter` so that the program has somewhere to display the objects in your program.

Make sure you include the underscore (_) after the named variable `from_`. In Python, `from` means something entirely different than `from_`. It might look almost identical to us as people but, as you know, computers aren't people! Computers take things very literally and to a computer `from` is as different to `from_` as cats are to cakes.

The line of the program that creates the slider is pretty straightforward. The `Scale()` function creates a new slider. As with all other widgets in Tkinter, the first argument tells the program which surface the object will be placed upon. The `from_` argument states the lowest value on the slider. Make sure you remember to include the underscore. In your program, the lowest value is 0, as `from_=0`. Likewise, the highest value on the slider is set using the `to` argument. This program sets the highest value of the slider to 100, as `to=100`. You can of course change these values to whatever integer value you want. Do you think the slider will work with floats (that is, numbers with decimal places)?

Keywords in Python are a set of reserved words which have a specific purpose in the programming language. As they are reserved, these words can't be used as the names of variables, functions or arguments. For example, the `if` keyword is used to create `if` statements so you can't use `if` as the name of a variable. Table 4-1 includes the list of Python keywords for Python 2.7.

Table 4-1	A List of Python Keywords That Cannot Be Used for the Names of Variables, Functions and Arguments			
and	del	for	is	raise
assert	elif	from	lambda	return
break	else	global	not	try
class	except	if	or	while
continue	exec	import	pass	
def	finally	in	print	

Can you work out how to print the value of the slider or use it to update the value in a text box? Think about the things you did in Adventure 3 for hints on how to do this.

Now that you are acquainted with the slider, you're going to learn about how computers represent colours and how to create a `canvas` object in `Tkinter`. The canvas will be used to display colours.

How Colours Work on Computers and as Hexadecimal Values

As you may know, all colours are made by mixing the three primary colours: red, green and blue. By mixing different levels of these three base colours together you can make any colour you want. For example, if you mix a lot of red with a little bit of green and a lot of blue you can make a bright purple.

You may be used to mixing colours with paint using red, yellow and blue paints. However, this is slightly different on computers. The colour green is used instead of yellow as the light from your computer monitor mixes colours differently to paint. Therefore, the three primary colours on computer monitors are red, green and blue.

A **pixel** is a tiny dot on your computer monitor. Everything that is displayed on your monitor is made up of lots of pixels. The colour for each pixel is set by mixing the three primary colours: red, green and blue.

For every colour, your computer needs a way to represent how much red, green and blue to mix together. There are a few ways of doing this. The first way is to use the numbers 0 to 255 to state how much red, green and blue are mixed together. For example, to make a very strong green colour you would have a red value of 0, a green value of 255 and a blue value of 0. You can combine any values for the three primary colours. For example, you could have a red value of 128, a green value of 37 and a blue value of 243 or anything else you want.

Another way to represent colour is to use hexadecimal colour values. Colours are still made up from a mixture of red, green and blue values, but the values are written slightly differently. Instead of using the numbers 0 to 255, hexadecimal values use a combination of letters and numbers. For example, a strong green colour has a value of #00FF00. To work out the value of each colour you need to understand how counting in hexadecimal works.

Let's look at how you normally count. You can probably count from 0 to 9. You start on 0. Then 1 comes before 2, 3 then 4 come next and so on until your reach 9. After 9, you reach the number 10; you start increasing the number on the right again so you have 11, 12, 13 until you reach 19; then the number on the left changes again so you have 20. Each number that makes up a bigger number is called a digit. So the digits for 23 are 2 and 3. You count ten numbers (0-9) on the lowest digit before you increase the one to the left of it.

Hexadecimal counting is slightly different. You start on 0, 1 comes before 2, 3 before 4 and so on all the way up to 9. You might expect the number after 9 to be 10, but in hexadecimal it is A. The number after A is B, then C, D, E and finally F. If you were to convert the numbers A, B, C, D, E and F to numbers that you were used to, A would be the number 10, B would be 11, C 12, D 13, E 14 and F is 15. Once you've counted to F, the next number is 10. The hexadecimal value of 10 isn't 10, it's actually 16; this is because F is 15 and the number after F is 10. So 10 in hexadecimal is 16 in normal numbers.

After counting to 10 in hexadecimal you start again. The next number is 11, then 12, 13, 14, all the way to 19, then it's 1A, 1B, 1C, 1D, 1E and 1F. After that the next number is 20 (which is 32 in normal numbers). This pattern continues all the way to FF, which is the value 255 in normal numbers.

Hexadecimal is a numbering system that uses the numbers 0-9 and letters A-F for each digit. The letter A is the equivalent of the number 10, B = 11, C = 12, D = 13, E = 14 and F = 15.

A **hexadecimal colour code** uses hexadecimal numbers to represent colour values. Each primary colour on the computer—red, green and blue—is given a hexadecimal number between 00 and FF to state the intensity of that colour in the mix.

Getting back to colours, each colour that uses a hexadecimal colour code is a combination of three sets of hexadecimal values. For example a red value of FF, a blue value of 00 and a green value of FF would be written as #FF00FF. All hexadecimal colour codes have a hash symbol (#) at the start. The first pair of hexadecimal values is always red, the second is green and the third is blue.

A few important colours to know: the value of #FFFFFF is white, which is the maximum value you can have for a hexadecimal colour code. The opposite of white is black, which has the value of #000000 and is the smallest hexadecimal value for any colour code. A strong red is #FF0000, strong green #00FF00 and a strong blue is #0000FF.

Don't worry if this is a little confusing to begin with. Table 4-2 has example colours that are written in hexadecimal. There's also a program you'll learn about later that converts the numbers 0-255 into hexadecimal codes.

Table 4-2	A Selection of Colours and Their Hexadecimal Values		
Red	Green	Blue	White
#FF0000	#00FF00	#0000FF	#FFFFFF
Purple	Yellow	Turquoise	Black
#FF00FF	#FFFF00	#00FFFF	#000000
Light Blue	Orange	Pink	Light Grey
#AAAAFF	#FFAA00	#FF9696	#AAAAAA
Mint/Light Green	Light Brown	Rosy Red	Dark Grey
#DDFFFF	#A17840	#EF0B05	#333333

The best way to understand what is going on is to try it out for yourself. In the next part of your adventure you'll be introduced to the canvas object in Tkinter and use hexadecimal colour codes to change it.

Changing the Canvas Colour

The canvas in Tkinter is used for drawings and displaying images. In your colour picker program, you'll use the canvas as a large space to display your colour.

You've just been introduced to the canvas and how colours are represented in hexadecimal values, so you're now going to create a short program that combines the two to display a colour in a window.

1. First open IDLE and create a new file editor.

2. Save the program as canvasColour.py in the Adventure 4 folder.

3. Copy these lines of code into the file editor:

```
import Tkinter as tk
window = tk.Tk()


colour = "#FF0000"
```

4. Add the next line of code to your program:

```
canvas = tk.Canvas(window, height=300, width=300, bg=colour)
```

5. Finally add the last two lines of the program into the file editor:

```
canvas.pack()
window.mainloop()
```

6. Save the program and run it using Run⇨Run Module.

7. The window should appear, filled with a red square (see Figure 4-3).

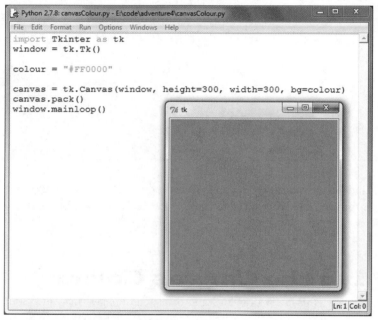

FIGURE 4-3 A Tkinter canvas

You can change the colour of the background by changing the value of the colour variable. For example, to change the square to black you would change the value of the hexadecimal colour code in the string to #000000. Use Table 4-2 to help you or try making your own using hexadecimal values.

Try using other colours and experiment with creating your own.

You're familiar with the first two lines of the program. The third line stores a string with a hexadecimal colour value in the `colour` variable. Remember that each pair of characters represents the amount of much red, green, or blue light that is mixed to result in the final colour, and that each character has a value between 0–9 and A–F. Can you remember the colour that this hexadecimal code represents?

The next line of code creates the `canvas` object. The width and height of the canvas is set using the `width` and `height` arguments. Both of these are set to 300 pixels in this example, so the canvas will be square. The `bg` argument sets the background colour of the canvas. It expects a hexadecimal colour code stored in a string. In this example, the `colour` variable, which stores a hexadecimal colour value in a string, is given for the value.

Making the Colour Picker

For a video that walks you through the steps of making a colour picker, visit the companion website at www.wiley.com/go/adventuresinpython. Click the Videos tab and select the appropriate file.

The first larger program you are going to create in this adventure is the colour picker. The program will use three sliders to create a colour. Once the main part of the program is done, you'll add a text box so that you can copy and use your colours in other programs.

1. First things first. Open IDLE and create a new file editor using File↪New Window.

2. Save the program as `colourPicker.py` in the `Adventure 4` folder.

3. Add the two lines that are used to import the `Tkinter` commands into Python and set up `Tkinter`:

```
import Tkinter as tk
window = tk.Tk()
```

4. Next you need to add a function that tells Python what to do when a slider is updated:

```
def sliderUpdate(source):
    red = redSlider.get()
    green = greenSlider.get()
    blue = blueSlider.get()

colour = "#%02x%02x%02x" % (red, green, blue)
canvas.config(bg=colour)
```

5. The next part of the program creates the sliders and the canvas. Add it to your program below the function:

```
redSlider = tk.Scale(window, from_=0, to=255, ↵
  command=sliderUpdate)
greenSlider = tk.Scale(window, from_=0, to=255, ↵
  command=sliderUpdate)
blueSlider = tk.Scale(window, from_=0, to=255, ↵
  command=sliderUpdate)

canvas = tk.Canvas(window, width=200, height=200)
```

6. Instead of using pack() you can use a grid so that the objects are aligned next to each other as well as on the top or below. Add the following code to arrange the sliders and canvas in a grid:

```
redSlider.grid(row=1, column=1)
greenSlider.grid(row=1, column=2)
blueSlider.grid(row=1, column=3)
canvas.grid(row=2, column=1, columnspan=3)
```

7. Finally add the mainloop() function to the program:

```
tk.mainloop()
```

8. Now click on Run⇨Run Module to run the program.

9. The window will appear and you'll see the three sliders. Slide them up and down to change the colour.

10. Figure 4-4 shows the colour picker program working.

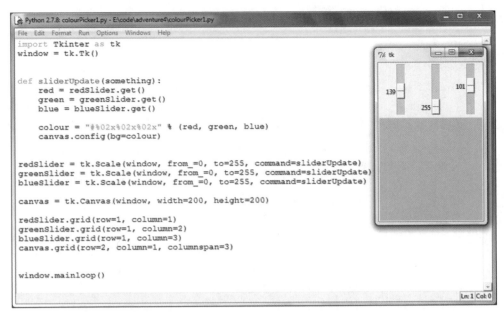

FIGURE 4-4 The colour picker GUI

The code shown in the figure:

```python
import Tkinter as tk
window = tk.Tk()

def sliderUpdate(something):
    red = redSlider.get()
    green = greenSlider.get()
    blue = blueSlider.get()

    colour = "#%02x%02x%02x" % (red, green, blue)
    canvas.config(bg=colour)

redSlider = tk.Scale(window, from_=0, to=255, command=sliderUpdate)
greenSlider = tk.Scale(window, from_=0, to=255, command=sliderUpdate)
blueSlider = tk.Scale(window, from_=0, to=255, command=sliderUpdate)

canvas = tk.Canvas(window, width=200, height=200)

redSlider.grid(row=1, column=1)
greenSlider.grid(row=1, column=2)
blueSlider.grid(row=1, column=3)
canvas.grid(row=2, column=1, columnspan=3)

window.mainloop()
```

DIGGING INTO THE CODE

There are a couple of new things going on here in the `sliderUpdate()` function. Let's take them one at a time. The first line gets the value of the slider used to set the amount of red in the final colour.

The program then does the same for the green and blue values.

The `colour` variable converts the hexadecimal values for all three colours into a single hexadecimal colour value and stores it in a string. The final line of the function updates the background colour of the canvas using the `colour` variable.

Like the button object that you were introduced to in Adventure 3, the `Scale` object can also use the command argument. The command argument states a function that will be run when the slider is updated. In this code the function is `sliderUpdate()`, so the function that you created at the start of the program will run whenever the sliders are moved. This will change the colour of the canvas as the slider moves. An alternative would have been to use a button to update the canvas, but this would mean that the colour wouldn't update automatically when the sliders move.

The highest value for each of the sliders is 255. This is the equivalent of the hexadecimal value of FF, but in decimal numbers, which are the type of numbers that you are used to. The program does this conversion for you.

continued

continued

Hexadecimal is used in nearly all programming languages and applications, not just Python.

Next, the program needs to place the objects on the window. So far you have used the `pack()` function to do this, but this function places all of the objects on top of each other, which doesn't look great.

The `grid()` function takes two arguments, `row` and `column`. The row states where the object will be vertically. Objects in row 2 will be below objects in row 1. Columns state where the items will be horizontally. The higher the value of column, the farther to the right it will be.

The sliders are placed on the first row, each in a separate column. The canvas is in the second row so that it is below the sliders. The canvas starts in column 1 and, using the `columnspan` argument, it fills three columns so that it spreads below all three sliders. It would just make the first column really big if the `columnspan` argument was left out, which would look terrible.

Adding a Text Box

Now that you have your colour mixer program working, it would be useful to be able to copy the hexadecimal colour code so that you can use it in other programs.

With just a few lines of Python code you can add a text box to the bottom of the window so that you can copy the hexadecimal colour values into other programs and applications. Here's how:

1. Make sure you have the code for your colour picker program open in IDLE. You should have saved it as `colourPicker.py` in the `Adventure 4` folder.

2. At the end of the `sliderUpdate()` function, add these two lines. They will update the text box to include the hexadecimal colour value whenever a slider is updated:

```
hexText.delete(0, tk.END)
hexText.insert(0, colour)
```

3. Below the line that begins with `canvas = tk.Canvas` add the following line of code to create the text box:

```
hexText = tk.Entry(window)
```

4. Find this line of code in your program:

```
window.mainloop()
```

5. Above it, add this line of Python code to add the text box to the window using the grid system:

```
hexText.grid(row=3, column=1, columnspan=3)
```

6. Save the program and run it using Run⇨Run Module.

You should notice that the window now has an additional text box at the bottom. Try moving the sliders and you will notice that the value in the text box changes. This value will be the same as the colour used for the background of the canvas.

Figure 4-5 shows the program with the added text box.

You can copy this value and use it in other programs and applications. For example, if you are using graphics software to draw a picture you can use it to select a colour for the paintbrush. You can also use it to set the colour of different things in your Python programs.

FIGURE 4-5 The colour picker with the text box

Creating a Click Speed Game

For a video that shows this game in action, visit the companion website at www.wiley.com/go/adventuresinpython. Click the Videos tab and select the appropriate file.

In the final stage of this adventure in GUIs, You're going to create a small but perfectly formed game. The aim of the game is to click as fast as possible. The time it takes to click 100 times is calculated by the game and displayed in the GUI. This program demonstrates how different GUI components can be combined with time and a count to create a game.

This GUI includes a button, a slider that records the number of times you've clicked the button and a label that shows the number of seconds it took to click 100 times.

1. Open IDLE and create a new window with File⇨New Window.

2. Save the program as `clickSpeed.py` in the `Adventure 4` folder.

3. Add the following lines of code to allow your program to use `Tkinter` and the time module:

```
import Tkinter as tk
import time
window = tk.Tk()
```

4. Next add these variables below the code. The first variable records the number of times you have clicked a button, the start variable records the time you started clicking, and the goal variable is the number of times you need to click in order to complete the game:

```
clicks = 0
start = 0
goal = 100
```

5. This function runs code whenever the button is clicked. The global expression before the variables means that this function can change the value of these variables. Add the first three lines of the function to your program:

```
def buttonClick():
    global clicks
    global start
```

6. The next part of the function checks how many times you've clicked. If you haven't started clicking, it will record the start time and add 1 to the clicks variable. If the number of clicks is greater than or equal to the maximum number of clicks it will calculate how long it took to click that many times, display the score and reset the clicks to 0. If the number of clicks is greater than 0 and less than the goal, then the number of clicks will be increased by 1. The last line sets the slider to the number of times the button has been clicked. Add these lines of code now:

```
    if clicks == 0:
            start = time.time()
            clicks = clicks + 1
        elif clicks + 1 >= goal:
        score = time.time() - start
            label.config(text="Time: " + str(score))
            clicks = 0
```

```
        else:
            clicks = clicks + 1
        slider.set(clicks)
```

7. These lines of code create the button, slider and label. Add them to your program:

```
button = tk.Button(window, text="Click me", ↵
  command=buttonClick)
slider = tk.Scale(window, from_=0, to=goal)
label = tk.Label(window)
```

8. Finally the button, slider and label are added to the window and the window starts. Add these lines of code to your program:

```
button.pack()
slider.pack()
label.pack()
window.mainloop()
```

9. Save your program and click Run➪Run Module.

10. Your program should look something like Figure 4-6.

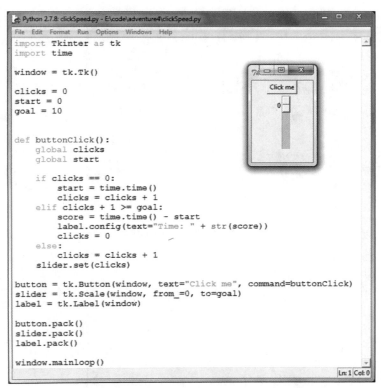

FIGURE 4-6 The click speed game

Python Command Quick Reference Table

Command	Description
`tk.Scale()`	The `scale()` function is used to create a slider in `Tkinter`. Using the named arguments `from_` and `to`, you can set the maximum and minimum values of the slider.
`'#FFFFFF'`	To create colours in Tkinter, you store them in strings. A hash sign (#) goes at the start of the string and the colour value is determined by the six numbers and letters in the string.
`tk.Canvas()`	The `canvas` function creates a canvas in `Tkinter`. The canvas can be used for drawing. In this adventure you used the canvas to display a colour.
`config()`	The `config()` function is used to change the settings of `Tkinter` objects. For example, you can use it to change the colour of the background of a canvas or the text on a button.
`grid()`	This is used to arrange `Tkinter` objects in a grid.

`colour =`
`  "#%02x%02x%02x" %`
`  (red, green, blue)`
	This code is used to format red, green and blue integer values to as a hexadecimal value stored in a string.

Achievement Unlocked: **Accomplished creator of advanced GUIs with** `Tkinter`.

Next Adventure

Congratulations! You've completed your adventures with `Tkinter`, during which you've learned how to create GUIs with it. In this leg of your journey, you've explored sliders and colours to create some really cool programs.

In your next adventure, you'll start to get to grips with a large and useful Python library called `PyGame`. As it's name suggests, you can use `PyGame` to create games, but it's also really flexible and can be used for creating images, animations and a whole load of other things as well. You'll start by familiarising yourself with drawing shapes and making some basic animations.

Adventure 5
Drawing Shapes with PyGame

PYTHON IS USED for a huge variety of things. So far, you've used it to create a text-based interface, drawings with the `turtle` module and GUIs with the `Tkinter` module. In this and the following adventures, you will learn to use `PyGame`. As its name suggests, `PyGame` is a module in Python that can be used to make games. `PyGame` is a very versatile module and is also very good for creating drawings, animations, sounds, interactive art and lots of other things.

As `PyGame` is a Python module, you can use it alongside all of the Python that you've learned so far.

In this adventure, you're going to use `PyGame` to create some animations. In later adventures, you'll build upon the things you've learned here, building up to the final adventure in which you will build a fantastic game.

Installing PyGame

Before starting this adventure, you need to have `PyGame` installed on your computer. Unless you're using a Raspberry Pi, `PyGame` probably isn't pre-installed on your computer. Before you go any further, follow the installation instructions in the Appendix for `PyGame` on your computer.

My First PyGame

For a video that walks you through the process of creating these shapes in PyGame, visit the companion website at www.wiley.com/go/adventuresinpython. Click the Videos tab and select the appropriate file.

In PyGame, you can create shapes and build upon them to create images, animations and games. In this adventure, you will start by learning how to create shapes in PyGame. You'll then combine the shapes to create images and animations.

This first program is really straightforward. All it will do is draw a circle. You can see what this will look like in Figure 5-1.

FIGURE 5-1 Your first PyGame program

1. Open a new file editor in IDLE by clicking File⇨New Window.

2. On the first line of the file, you will need to import and initialise PyGame. Copy these two lines of code to do this:

```
import pygame
pygame.init()
```

3. Copy these two lines of code to set up the window size:

```
windowSize = [400, 300]
screen = pygame.display.set_mode(windowSize)
```

4. Next, you need to set the title of the window, which you do by using `set_caption()`. In this case we have called it `Circles`, but you can use any string you like to set the title of the window. Copy this line into the file editor:

```
pygame.display.set_caption("Circles")
```

5. Colours in `PyGame` can be represented using hexadecimal values, which you have already used for `Tkinter` in the previous adventure. To use a hexadecimal colour in `PyGame` you use the code `pygame.color.Color('#FFFFFF')` and change the colour argument in the brackets to whatever you want. Copy this code into your file editor:

```
colour = pygame.color.Color('#FFFFFF')
```

6. Copy this part of the code to make the program loop:

```
done = False
while not done:
```

7. To draw a circle in `PyGame` you use the `circle()` function. This takes four arguments:

   - The surface that you want to put it on, in this case, "screen".

   - The colour, for which the variable white has been used.

   - The coordinates for the centre of the circle.

   - The radius of the circle. The radius, as you probably know, is the distance between the centre of the circle and the edge of the circle.

   The `flip()` function then updates the window to include all shapes that were drawn to it. Copy this code (and remember to indent):

```
pygame.draw.circle(screen, colour, [200, 150], 50)
pygame.display.flip()
```

8. In order for the program to close when the Close button is clicked, you need to include code in your program to tell Python what to do. The four lines of code at the end of the program allow the window to be closed. The `for` gets all of the events, such as attempts to close the window. The `if` statement checks if any of these events are a request to close the window. If they are, `done` is set to `True`, which will cause the main game loop to terminate. The last line, which is outside the main game loop, quits `PyGame`. Copy these four lines into the file editor (remember to indent):

```
        for event in pygame.event.get():
            if event.type == pygame.QUIT:
                done = True
pygame.quit()
```

9. Run your program by going to Run⇨Run Program. Create a new folder called `Adventure 5`. Save the program as `circle.py`.

10. You can see the result of the program in Figure 5-1.

Getting `PyGame` running to draw a single shape does take a few lines of code. However, it doesn't get much more complicated to draw multiple shapes in the same window. You are probably already beginning to imagine the exciting things you can do with this!

DIGGING INTO THE CODE

You may recognise the `import` part of this code, as you used something similar when importing the `turtle` module in the previous adventure. It allows you to use all of the `PyGame` commands in the module. The `init()` part of this initialises `PyGame` and prepares it so that you can use it.

`PyGame` creates a new window when it runs. The first line of this code creates a variable where you store the size of the window you want to use, in this case 400 pixels by 300 pixels. The next line creates a screen surface with the dimensions that you just stored in the `windowSize` variables. A surface in `PyGame` is used to place drawings and pictures onto. Think of it as a canvas on which `PyGame` draws.

To make the window stay open, a loop is used. The `done` variable stores a **boolean** to indicate whether or not your program is done. When it is not done, the loop will repeat. The `done` variable will be `True` when we try to close the window (the code for this is added a bit further on in the program). This `while` loop is called a game loop as the bits that make games work are inside of it.

This program features a special type of `while` loop that is often called a game loop. Loops, as you know, are used to repeat code. Game loops are `while` loops that are used to manage specific aspects of video games. In particular, they are used to animate frames in the game and check if the player has given any commands to the game using the keyboard or mouse. You'll find out how to create animations later in this adventure and will learn how to use the keyboard and mouse with `PyGame` later in the book. Even though there aren't any animations in this program as the circle stays still, the code is arranged in a way that will be developed later to include animations.

Booleans are a data type in Python that have values of either `True` or `False`.

Creating Rectangles

There are a number of shapes that can be drawn in PyGame. You've already seen how to draw a circle. Creating other shapes isn't that different to creating a circle. You're now going to look at how to create a rectangle and then try out a couple of programs that use rectangles.

Shapes are very versatile when creating programs. They can be used in games and animations for various purposes. They can be combined in different ways to create new things like custom buttons, menus, backgrounds and a whole load of other things.

Creating a Rectangle

The code to create a basic rectangle is very straightforward. Let's look at it before moving onto some more complex programs that use rectangles:

```python
import pygame
pygame.init()

windowSize = [400, 300]
screen = pygame.display.set_mode(windowSize)
colour = pygame.color.Color('#0A32F4')

done = False
while not done:
    pygame.draw.rect(screen, colour, [10, 20, 30, 40])
    pygame.display.flip()
    for event in pygame.event.get():
        if event.type == pygame.QUIT:
            done = True
pygame.quit()
```

DIGGING INTO THE CODE

The function to create a rectangle is `rect()`. The function takes three arguments: the surface on which the shape will be displayed (in this case it is the screen surface); the colour, which is stored in the colour variable; and the coordinates, width and height of the rectangle. The coordinates represent the top-left corner of the rectangle. The other two numbers represent the width and height. For example, using the list [10, 20, 30, 40], one corner of the rectangle would be at the coordinates [10, 20], the width would be 30 and the height would be 40.

This code will generate a small blue rectangle in the top-left corner of the window, like in Figure 5-2.

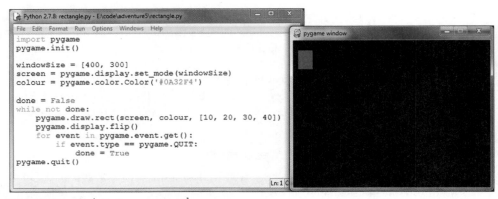

FIGURE 5-2 A PyGame rectangle

Want to try out the program? Just follow these steps:

1. Open IDLE and create a new window with File⇨New Window.

2. Save the program as `rectangle.py` in the `Adventure 5` folder.

3. Run the program with Run⇨Run Module.

A Rainbow of Rectangles

As with any Python code, small changes to the program will drastically change the effect of the program. For example, by adding an extra loop to the basic rectangle program, along with a few other lines of code, you can make a whole rainbow of stacked rectangles. In this next program you will do just that.

Figure 5-3 shows what the finished program looks like.

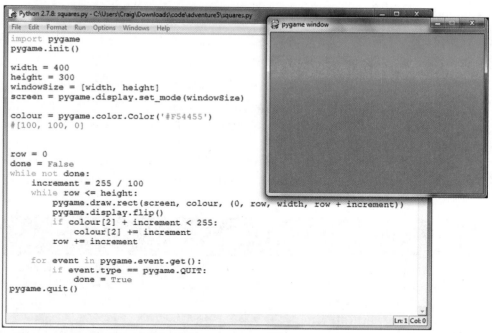

```
Python 2.7.8: squares.py - C:\Users\Craig\Downloads\code\adventure5\squares.py
File  Edit  Format  Run  Options  Windows  Help
import pygame
pygame.init()

width = 400
height = 300
windowSize = [width, height]
screen = pygame.display.set_mode(windowSize)

colour = pygame.color.Color('#F54455')
#[100, 100, 0]


row = 0
done = False
while not done:
    increment = 255 / 100
    while row <= height:
        pygame.draw.rect(screen, colour, (0, row, width, row + increment))
        pygame.display.flip()
        if colour[2] + increment < 255:
            colour[2] += increment
        row += increment

    for event in pygame.event.get():
        if event.type == pygame.QUIT:
            done = True
pygame.quit()
```

FIGURE 5-3 A gradient of rectangles

1. Open IDLE and create a new window using File⇨New Window.

2. Save the program as `rainbow.py` in the `Adventure 5` folder.

3. In the file editor, add the following code to set up PyGame and the window:

```
import pygame
pygame.init()

width = 400
height = 300
windowSize = [width, height]
screen = pygame.display.set_mode(windowSize)
```

4. The next bit of the code sets the starting colour of the rectangle:

```
colour = pygame.color.Color('#646400')
row = 0
done = False
while not done:
    increment = 255 / 100
```

5. Next add the following code to draw the rectangles. The `while` loop will stop drawing rectangles when they fill the screen. If this weren't included, the program would carry on drawing rectangles off the screen! Add the code now:

```
while row <= height:
    pygame.draw.rect(screen, colour, (0, row, width,
        row + increment))
```

```
        pygame.display.flip()
        if colour[2] + increment < 255:
            colour[2] += increment
        row += increment
```

6. Finally add this code to handle when the user wants to close the window:

```
    for event in pygame.event.get():
        if event.type == pygame.QUIT:
            done = True
pygame.quit()
```

7. Save and run the program with Run⇨Run Module.

DIGGING INTO THE CODE

The `colour` variable contains the starting colour of the first rectangle. The loop later in the program has a line that adds to this until the value reaches 255, which is the maximum value. The `row` variable is used to calculate the vertical position of the rectangle. This increases every time the loop repeats, in order to place the rectangles below one another. The `increment` variable determines how much the colour and rectangle will increase each time the loop repeats. The number 100 means that 100 rectangles will be displayed. Decreasing this number means there will be fewer rectangles and increasing it means there will be more rectangles.

In this code the values of red, green and blue are stored in a single list, instead of as individual values. To access or change the colour values, the code uses the value of `colour[0]` for red, `colour[1]` for green and `colour[2]` for blue.

Trying changing the starting colour of the program. At the moment, the blue is increased each time the loop repeats. As the blue increases in this program the overall mixed colour changes from red to pink, as the values for red and green are mixed in with the changing level of blue. You can change it to red by changing the code that says `colour[2]` to `colour[0]` or change it to green by changing the code to `colour[1]`.

This is the first time you've come across the `+=` operator in Python. This is a shorthand addition operator. It is a quick way to add a value to a variable. You are used to writing code like this to add a number to a variable and store it back in the same variable `row = row + 1`. The shorthand addition operator is an alternative to this and means you only have to write the variable name once like so: `row += 1`. There are also shorthand operators for subtraction (–), multiplication (*=) and division (/=).

Colour Grid

This next program creates a grid of randomly coloured squares. It uses the rectangle in PyGame. The program repeats over and over again, placing a randomly coloured square at a random position every time it loops. The random module is used to do this.

1. Open IDLE and click on File⇨New Window.

2. Save the program as randomGrid.py in the Adventure 5 folder.

3. Copy these lines of code into the file editor:

```
import random
import pygame
pygame.init()
```

4. The PyGame Clock() is similar to the time module. It is used to control the speed that the while loop in the program runs. You will see how this works later in the program. Add this code to your program:

```
width = 400
height = 300
windowSize = [width, height]
screen = pygame.display.set_mode(windowSize)
clock = pygame.time.Clock()

sqrW = width / 10
sqrH = height / 10
```

5. The next part of the program will draw the squares at random positions:

```
done = False
while not done:
    red = random.randrange(0, 256)
    green = random.randrange(0, 256)
    blue = random.randrange(0, 256)

    x = random.randrange(0, width, sqrW)
    y = random.randrange(0, width, sqrH)
    pygame.draw.rect(screen, (red, green, blue), (x, y,
      sqrW, sqrH))

    pygame.display.flip()

    for event in pygame.event.get():
        if event.type == pygame.QUIT:
            done = True
    clock.tick(10)
pygame.quit()
```

6. Save the program and run it. You should see something that looks like Figure 5-4.

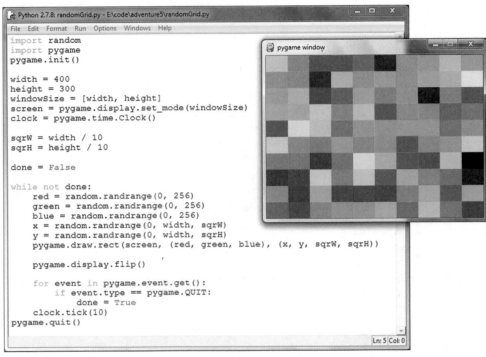

```
Python 2.7.8: randomGrid.py - E:\code\adventure5\randomGrid.py
File  Edit  Format  Run  Options  Windows  Help
import random
import pygame
pygame.init()

width = 400
height = 300
windowSize = [width, height]
screen = pygame.display.set_mode(windowSize)
clock = pygame.time.Clock()

sqrW = width / 10
sqrH = height / 10

done = False

while not done:
    red = random.randrange(0, 256)
    green = random.randrange(0, 256)
    blue = random.randrange(0, 256)
    x = random.randrange(0, width, sqrW)
    y = random.randrange(0, width, sqrH)
    pygame.draw.rect(screen, (red, green, blue), (x, y, sqrW, sqrH))

    pygame.display.flip()

    for event in pygame.event.get():
        if event.type == pygame.QUIT:
            done = True
    clock.tick(10)
pygame.quit()
                                                          Ln: 5  Col: 0
```

FIGURE 5-4 The colour grid

DIGGING INTO THE CODE

The `randrange()` function can take a third argument that makes the random numbers it generates go up in steps. For example, using 5 as the third argument, like so: `randrange(0, 100, 5)`, would make any random number that goes up steps of five between 0 and 95, including 5, 10, 15, 20, 25, 30 and so on. In the random square grid program, this number is used so that the squares stick to a grid.

This program uses a slightly different way to represent numbers. Instead of using hexadecimal values to store the colour, the red, green and blue parts of the colour have a number between 0 and 255. This still gives you access to exactly the same colours as using a hexadecimal value, it just means the values are represented differently.

The `clock.tick()` line of code controls the speed of the loop. It determines the number of times a second the loop will repeat. In this example the loop will repeat ten times a second.

Creating Ellipses

Ellipses are like circles only elongated, with their width not the same the whole way around (think of an egg). In PyGame you can create ellipses in the same way that you'd create any other shape.

Wobbling Circle

For a video that walks you through the process of creating this wobbling circle, visit the companion website at www.wiley.com/go/adventuresinpython. Click the Videos tab and select the appropriate file.

You are now going to create a small animation featuring a wobbling circle. The program will use an ellipse, and the height and width of the ellipse will change during the animation.

1. As usual, open IDLE and click on File↷New Window.

2. Save the program as wobble.py in the Adventure 5 folder.

3. Start by adding these lines of code to the program:

```
import math
import pygame
pygame.init()
```

4. Add these lines to set up the window:

```
windowSize = [400, 300]
screen = pygame.display.set_mode(windowSize)
clock = pygame.time.Clock()
```

5. The next bit of code determines the length and width of the ellipse, as well as the x and y coordinates where the ellipse will be placed. You calculate the x and y values by taking half of the height or width of the screen, then subtracting half the height or width of the shape. Add the code now:

```
width = 200
height = 200
x = windowSize[0] / 2 - width / 2
y = windowSize[1] / 2 - height / 2
colour = pygame.color.Color('#57B0F6')
black = pygame.color.Color('#000000')
```

6. The next part of the program draws the ellipse. Each time the loop repeats, it changes the width and height of the shape using the `cos()` and `sin()` functions. Both of these functions use their arguments to generate waves. As the values increase, the returned values make a smooth wave. This is useful as the ellipse will change size in a continuous and smooth motion. The x and y positions are also adjusted to compensate for the change in width and height so that the shape stays in the centre of the window. Add this code:

```
count = 0
done = False

while not done:
    screen.fill(black)
    pygame.draw.ellipse(screen, colour, [x, y, width,
      height])
    width += math.cos(count) * 10
    x -= (math.cos(count) * 10) / 2
    height += math.sin(count) * 10
    y -= (math.sin(count) * 10) / 2
    count += 0.5

    pygame.display.flip()

    for event in pygame.event.get():
        if event.type == pygame.QUIT:
            done = True
    clock.tick(24)
    pygame.quit()
```

7. Run the program with Run⇨Run Module.

The program will create a wobbling circle and should look something like Figure 5-5.

CHALLENGE

Can you change the program to use a rectangle instead of an ellipse? Try changing the program so that the colour of the shape changes, too.

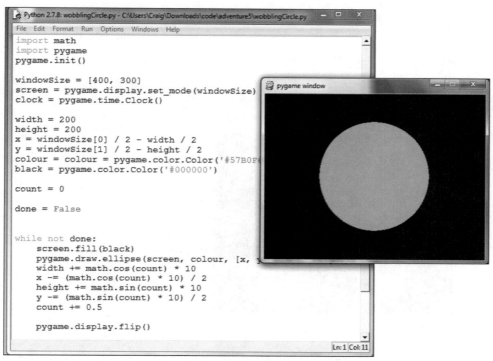

```
Python 2.7.8: wobblingCircle.py - C:\Users\Craig\Downloads\code\adventure5\wobblingCircle.py

File  Edit  Format  Run  Options  Windows  Help

import math
import pygame
pygame.init()

windowSize = [400, 300]
screen = pygame.display.set_mode(windowSize)
clock = pygame.time.Clock()

width = 200
height = 200
x = windowSize[0] / 2 - width / 2
y = windowSize[1] / 2 - height / 2
colour = colour = pygame.color.Color('#57B0F
black = pygame.color.Color('#000000')

count = 0

done = False

while not done:
    screen.fill(black)
    pygame.draw.ellipse(screen, colour, [x,
    width += math.cos(count) * 10
    x -= (math.cos(count) * 10) / 2
    height += math.sin(count) * 10
    y -= (math.sin(count) * 10) / 2
    count += 0.5

    pygame.display.flip()
                                                Ln: 1 Col: 11
```

FIGURE 5-5 A single frame of the wobbling circle animation

Saving Your Images

Saving images that you've created in PyGame is very straightforward. To save a PyGame surface, you only have to use this one line of Python code:

```
pygame.image.save(surface, filename)
```

For example, if you want to save the surface called screen in a file called squares.png, you use the following line of code:

```
pygame.image.save(screen, "squares.png")
```

Saving a Single Image

In two of the programs you created earlier in this adventure, you made a grid of randomly coloured squares and a gradient. These two images are suitable for saving, as they are not animations. Although you can save a single image from the wobbling circle program if you want, it is probably not worth it—because it is an animation, all you'd be able to save is an image of the ellipse.

To save an image generated in the two earlier programs, simply add this statement on the second last line of the program before `pygame.quit()`:

```
pygame.image.save(screen, "squares.png")
```

To change the filename, you change the text in the string. Figure 5-6 shows an image from the colour grid program.

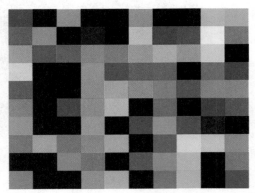

FIGURE 5-6 A saved image from the colour grid program

Saving a Series of Images

It may not be worth saving a single image from an animation, but it might be more useful to save a series of images from an animation. To do this, you save the surface each time the loop repeats.

One way of doing this is to put the `save()` function by itself in the loop. This will save the surface for each frame in the animation.

Here is part of the wobbling circle program, modified to save the image in each frame. It also includes a `fileNo` variable so that the images are numbered in order when they are saved:

```
fileNo = 0
while not done:
    screen.fill(black)
    pygame.draw.ellipse(screen, colour, [x, y, width, height])
    width += math.cos(count) * 10
    x -= (math.cos(count) * 10) / 2
    height += math.sin(count) * 10
    y -= (math.sin(count) * 10) / 2
    count += 0.5

    pygame.display.flip()
    pygame.image.save(screen, "circle" + str(fileNo) + ".png")
    fileNo += 1
```

One problem with this method of saving the program is that it will create a lot of images very quickly. You can add an `if` statement, however, so that only a certain number of images are saved. This code modifies the last two lines of the previous program and adds an `if` statement so that it only saves 20 images:

```
if fileNo < 20:
    pygame.image.save(screen, "circle" + str(fileNo) +
        ".png")
    fileNo += 1
```

Python Command Quick Reference Table

Command	Description
`import pygame`	Imports the contents of the PyGame library so that you can use it in your program.
`pygame.init`	Initialises PyGame and allows you to subsequently use PyGame functions, such as functions that set the window size or places shapes on the PyGame window.
`pygame.display.set_mode()`	Sets the size of a PyGame window and creates a surface onto which shapes and other things can be placed.
`pygame.display.set_caption()`	Sets the title of a PyGame window.
`draw.circle()`	Draws a circle on a PyGame surface.
`display.flip()`	Updates the window to include any shapes you've drawn.
`pygame.event.get()`	Checks for events such as keypresses and closing the window. Returns the events as a list.
`event.type`	Gets the type of the event, such as a keypress or the window closing.
`event.QUIT`	Used to check if an event was to quit the window.
`pygame.quit()`	Quits PyGame.
`draw.rect()`	Draws a rectangle on a PyGame surface.
`pygame.color.Color('#FFFFFF')`	Creates a colour that PyGame can use.
`time.Clock()`	Creates a clock that can return the time and control the frames per second of a loop.
`clock.tick()`	Controls the number of frames per second of the PyGame program.
`draw.ellipse()`	Draws an ellipse in PyGame
`math.sin()`	Calculates the sine of a number. This can be used to generate wiggly lines when plotted on a graph.
`math.cos()`	Generates the cosine of a number. This can also be used to create slightly different wiggly numbers.
`image.save()`	Saves a PyGame surface to a file.
`variable += 1`	The shorthand addition operator adds a value to a variable.

Achievement Unlocked: **Expert creator of shapes with** PyGame.

Next Adventure

Excellent! You've completed your first adventure in PyGame. You can now create shapes in PyGame and also make some basic animations. This is where the fun starts. With PyGame your imagination can run riot. It allows you to use software to do everything from designing games to making your own musical instruments— and these are just some of the things you'll learn in future adventures.

In the next adventure, you'll learn how to make an actual game with PyGame.

Adding Keyboard Input with PyGame

WHEN YOU'RE PLAYING computer games on your PC, one of the ways you can give the game commands is via the keyboard. You use different keys to give different commands—for example, you usually use the W, A, S and D keys to move the player around the game.

In this adventure you'll learn how to use the keyboard with PyGame. You'll also make a game in which, for the first time, you'll move a player around the window. Okay—your player is just a dot on the screen at this stage, but it's a good start! As the program develops throughout the adventure, you'll add extra features like a ball that your player can "kick," a goal and a points system.

The gameplay and graphics in this game are very simple, so during the adventure you may want to add more features to the game, like better graphics. Try using some of the things you learned in Adventure 5 to add that little bit extra to the game. You can also come back to the game and improve it after you've learned more in later adventures. You'll be learning lots in the sound adventure in Adventure 9, for example, so you can add sound to the game once you know how to do that.

Using Keyboard Input

For a video that walks you through the steps of using this keyboard input, visit the companion website at www.wiley.com/go/adventuresinpython. Click the Videos tab and select the appropriate file.

Using the keyboard with a PyGame program is very straightforward. When you press a key on PyGame it adds it to a list of the keys that you've pressed. By checking which keys are in this list, you can make your program do different things.

Let's have a look at an example to understand this better:

1. Open IDLE and create a new file with File ⇨New Window. Create a new folder and call it Adventure 6. Save the program in the folder as keyboardExample.py.

2. Add this code to the file to set up the program and the window:

```
import pygame
pygame.init()
# Window setup
size = [400, 300]
screen = pygame.display.set_mode(size)
clock = pygame.time.Clock()
```

3. Next, you're going to add a game loop to the program. This type of loop is called a game loop, as it handles all of the action in the game. Add this code to your program:

```
# Game loop
done = False
while not done:
```

4. Next, your program needs to check for keypresses and decide what to do with them. Add this code to your program:

```
    keys = pygame.key.get_pressed()

    # Display a message when the w key is pressed
    if keys[pygame.K_w]:
        print "Hello"
```

5. Finally, you need to manage the player, close the window and set the frames per second. Add this code to your file:

```
    for event in pygame.event.get():
        if event.type == pygame.QUIT:
            done = True
    clock.tick(32)
pygame.quit()
```

6. Save the program and run it using Run⇨Run Module.

7. When the program loads you should see a black screen. Press the w key. You should see "Hello" printed to the console, as in Figure 6-1.

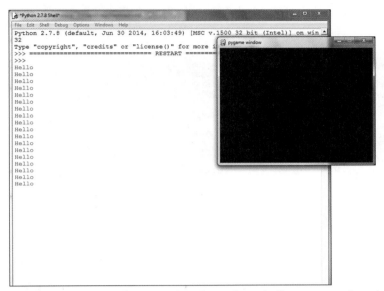

FIGURE 6-1 "Hello" is printed to the Python shell every time the w key is pressed.

DIGGING INTO THE CODE

This is the bit of the program that allows you to use the keyboard:

```
keys = pygame.key.get_pressed()

# Display a message when w key is pressed
if keys[pygame.K_w]:
    print "Hello"
```

There are several parts to this piece of code. The first bit, `keys = pygame.key.get_pressed()`, gets all of the keys that are currently pressed in the game and stores them as a list in the `keys` variable.

The next bit of code uses an `if` statement to check if one of the keys you pressed was the w key. The `pygame.K_w` tells PyGame that you are checking for the w key. You can change this to any key you want by changing the last letter of this. For example `pygame.K_t` would check if the t key was pressed.

Other Keys You Can Use

With PyGame you can use every key on the keyboard to control your programs. The letter keys are straightforward to work out. As you just did, all you have to do is replace the last letter of the code pygame.K_t with the letter you want to use. For example, if you wanted to use the x key, the code would be pygame.K_x. You don't have to stick to the letters though! Table 6-1 shows you a few of the other keys you can use and how to do it.

Table 6-1	Keyboard Control Codes in PyGame		
Key	**PyGame**	**Key**	**PyGame**
1	K_1	Escape	K_ESCAPE
Backspace	K_BACKSPACE	Right Shift	K_RSHIFT
Space	K_SPACE	Left Shift	K_LSHIFT
Enter	K_RETURN	Up	K_UP

You can also find a full list of PyGame keyboard keys at www.pygame.org/docs/refs/key.html.

Creating the Game

For a video that walks you through the steps of creating this game, visit the companion website at www.wiley.com/go/adventuresinpython. Click the Videos tab and select the appropriate file.

Now you're going to start making a little game in which you'll use the keyboard to move a player around the screen. The player won't be that complex—just a red dot on the screen. If you want to spend more time on this, why not think about what you learned in Adventure 5? You could always combine some shapes to make a much cooler picture of your player and use this instead of the red dot.

Figure 6-2 shows what the finished game will look like.

Once you've got the movement set up with the keyboard, you'll be adding more things to the game, like a ball and a goal. And an explosion!

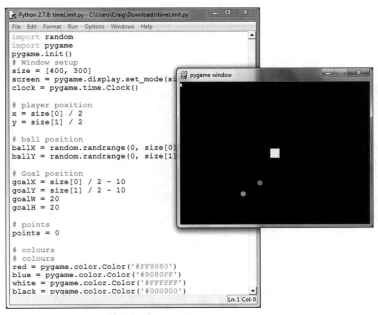

FIGURE 6-2 The finished game

This first part of the program will only move the player upwards. You'll add the code to move it in other directions afterwards.

Let's get going!

1. Open IDLE and create a new file with File⇨New Window. Save the program as `movementGame.py` in the `Adventure 6` folder.

2. In the new window, input the following code to set up the `PyGame` program:

    ```python
    import pygame
    pygame.init()
    # Window setup
    size = [400, 300]
    screen = pygame.display.set_mode(size)
    clock = pygame.time.Clock()
    ```

3. Next, you need your program to set a variable to represent the player's starting position. Set this as half the width of the window and half the height of the window:

    ```python
    # player position
    x = size[0] / 2
    y = size[1] / 2
    ```

4. Now you need to decide what colours you want to use for the player, ball, background and explosion. Add these three variables for the colours in your game:

```
# colours
red = pygame.color.Color('#FF8080')
blue = pygame.color.Color('#8080FF')
white = pygame.color.Color('#FFFFFF')
black = pygame.color.Color('#000000')
```

5. The next part of the program creates a game loop and draws black over the background. The game loop will also manage the keyboard inputs and drawing the game to the window. Add this to your program:

```
# Game loop
done = False
while not done:
    screen.fill(black)
```

6. The next part of the game loop needs to manage the keypresses for the player. This code checks that the w key is pressed and changes the y variable by -1 to change the position of the player. Add this to your code:

```
    keys = pygame.key.get_pressed()

    #player movement
    if keys[pygame.K_w]:
        y -= 1
```

7. Next, the program draws the player using the updated y variable and updates the window display. Add this to your program:

```
    # draw player
    pygame.draw.circle(screen, red, [x, y], 6)
    pygame.display.flip()
```

8. Finally, add this to code to your program to make sure the window can be closed and to limit the number of frames that are drawn per second:

```
    for event in pygame.event.get():
        if event.type == pygame.QUIT:
            done = True
    clock.tick(72)
pygame.quit()
```

9. Save the program and run it using Run⇨Run Module. You should get a window that looks like Figure 6-3, showing your player in position.

10. Press the w key and the player should move up the screen. If you hold down the key the player will keep moving until you stop pressing the key. If you keep going the player will move off the screen and never return!

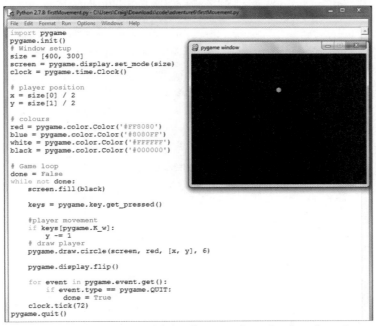

```python
import pygame
pygame.init()
# Window setup
size = [400, 300]
screen = pygame.display.set_mode(size)
clock = pygame.time.Clock()

# player position
x = size[0] / 2
y = size[1] / 2

# colours
red = pygame.color.Color('#FF8080')
blue = pygame.color.Color('#8080FF')
white = pygame.color.Color('#FFFFFF')
black = pygame.color.Color('#000000')

# Game loop
done = False
while not done:
    screen.fill(black)

    keys = pygame.key.get_pressed()

    #player movement
    if keys[pygame.K_w]:
        y -= 1
    # draw player
    pygame.draw.circle(screen, red, [x, y], 6)

    pygame.display.flip()

    for event in pygame.event.get():
        if event.type == pygame.QUIT:
            done = True
    clock.tick(72)
pygame.quit()
```

FIGURE 6-3 The small red dot will move upwards when the w key is pressed.

DIGGING INTO THE CODE

Your program is still far from complete, but you'll deal with that in a second.

The size of the window is stored in a list. A list is a way to store several values in a single variable. The values are put inside square brackets [ ] and separated by commas. Lists were introduced in Adventure 3.

The important bits are the x and y variables, which represent the player's position on the screen. The variables that store the player's position, x and y, are set to be at the centre of the window. To do this they access the width and height values stored in the size list and divide them by two. The first item in a list is always 0, so to access the width of the window the code uses `size[0]`. The second position of a list is 1 so the height of the window is `size[1]`.

If you haven't come across the x-axis and y-axis before now is your chance to find out about them. **Coordinates** are used to measure your position on a game

continued

continued

window. Your position from left to right is called the x-axis. The x-axis starts at 0 and as you move further to the right this number increases. So if you are at position 10 on the x-axis and move 5 further along the x-axis you will now be at position 15 on the x-axis. The y-axis works in exactly the same way, but from the top of the window to the bottom. The y-axis starts at 0 on the top of the window. As you move down, the value of the y-axis increases. So if you were at position 20 on the y-axis and moved 5 upwards you would now be at position 15 (20 − 5=15).

To move the player, your program changes these variables by adding and subtracting from them. At the moment this only works with the y variable by subtracting from it when the w key is pressed. In the next part of the program, you'll add the rest of the code to move in different directions.

The `screen.fill(black)` part of the code will clear the screen every frame. If this part of the code wasn't there, you'd be able to see all the positions that the player was in previously. This would create a long line, instead of showing the player as a dot.

Coordinates measure your position. They are used so that a number can be given to location. Coordinates are represented by two numbers, your x co-ordinate and y coordinate.

The **X Coordinate** measures your horizontal position (from left to right). The x coordinate starts at 0 at the left of the window and increases the farther right you move.

The **Y Coordinate** measures your vertical position (from top to bottom). The y coordinate starts at 0 at the top of the window and increases the farther down you go.

Introducing Full Movement

The game wouldn't be very good if your player could only move upwards. Time to fix that. In this part of your adventure, you'll add some code to enable the player to move up, down, left and right.

This will work when you press the w, a, s and d keys, which are normal movement controls for most modern computer games.

Let's go!

1. If `movementGame.py` is not already open, open it now.

2. Find the bit of the code that begins with the `#player movement` comment and the `if` statement that checks the w key is pressed. It should look like this:

```
#player movement
if keys[pygame.K_w]:
    y -= 1
```

3. Below that, add the following code to enable the player to move in the other directions:

```
if keys[pygame.K_s]:
    y += 1
if keys[pygame.K_a]:
    x -= 1
if keys[pygame.K_d]:
    x += 1
```

4. Save the program and run it with Run⇨Run Module.

5. When the program opens, you should now be able to move the player up, down, left and right by using the w, a, s and d keys (see Figure 6-4). Try out these keys to move the player. And here's an extra trick: you can also hold down two keys at a time to make the player move diagonally.

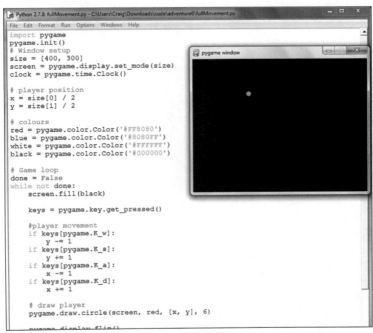

FIGURE 6-4 The small red dot will now move in different directions when you press the w, a, s and d keys.

Excellent! You've got a bit of movement in the game. But wait—at the moment the player disappears whenever you move them offscreen. We can't have that. You'll fix this in the next part of the program.

What happens when you press two keys at the same time? For example try pressing the w and a keys at the same time. Why do you think this happens?

Moving the Player Offscreen

At the moment, when you reach the edge of the display the player will disappear out of sight. This is because the player's co-ordinates, which are stored in the x and y variables, are bigger or smaller than the size of the screen.

This is quite straightforward to fix. To do it you'll add a function that checks whether the player is off the screen. If they are, it will teleport them to the opposite side of the screen. In other words if the player disappears off the top of the screen, they'll reappear at the bottom and vice versa. If they move off the right of the screen, they'll reappear on the left. Here's how:

1. Make sure you have the `movementGame.py` program open. If you don't, now's the time to open it.

2. In your program, find the following lines of code:

```
# Game loop
done = False
```

3. Above that code, add the following functions:

```
def checkOffScreenX(x):
    if x > size[0]:
        x = 0
    elif x < 0:
        x = size[0]
    return x

def checkOffScreenY(y):
    if y > size[1]:
        y = 0
    elif y < 0:
        y = size[1]
    return y
```

4. In order to make the function work, you'll need to add a call to it in the game loop. Find these lines in your code:

```
# draw player
pygame.draw.circle(screen, red, [x, y], 6)
```

5. Above that code, add the following code to run the code that checks whether the player has moved offscreen:

```
# Check off screen
x = checkOffScreenX(x)
y = checkOffScreenY(y)
```

6. Save the program and run it with Run⇨Run Module. When the window opens, move the player around with the w, a, s and d keys. Move the player off the top of the window; they should reappear at the bottom. Now try moving the player off the left, right and bottom of the screen and see what happens. Figure 6-5 shows screenshots before the player has moved offscreen and after they have reappeared.

FIGURE 6-5 The player is now able to move off the edge of the screen and reappear on the other side.

DIGGING INTO THE CODE

The checkOffScreenX() and checkOffScreenY() functions check whether the player has moved outside of the viewable area.

To check whether the player is offscreen on the x-axis, this code is used:

```
if x > size[0]:
    x = 0
elif x < 0:
    x = size[0]
```

continued

continued

This code checks if the x position is greater than the width of the window; in other words it checks whether the player has moved off the right of the screen. If the player has, it changes the x position to 0, which moves the player to the right of the screen. The second part checks whether the x position is less than 0; in other words, it checks whether the player has moved off the right of the screen. If the player has, it changes the x position to the width of the window, so it moves the player to the right side of the window. Similar code runs to check whether the player has moved off the y-axis.

The reason that the code is in two functions is so that it can be reused in other parts of the program, as you will see later in this adventure.

CRAIG SAYS...

Be careful when using x and y co-ordinates. If you accidentally mix them up, you can end up with a program that does some really weird things. For example, when I first made this program I accidentally put a y variable in the place of an x variable. The player and the ball became trapped on top of each other and started moving randomly around the window very quickly.

Adding the Ball

Now that you have a player that can move around the game, it would be great to have something they can interact with. In this part of the adventure, you'll add a ball to the game for the player to kick around. You'll later add a goal for the player to kick the ball into.

Your first task is to set the ball at a random position in the game and draw it:

1. In your `movementGame.py` program, add this line of code to the first line of the program. This will let your program use random numbers:

```
import random
```

2. Next, find the code in your program that sets the player's position. It should look like this:

```
# player position
x = size[0] / 2
y = size[1] / 2
```

3. Below it add the following code to set the position of the ball to a random location:

```
# ball position
ballX = random.randrange(0, size[0])
ballY = random.randrange(0, size[1])
```

4. Finally, you need to draw the ball in the game loop. Find the lines of code that set the player's position:

```
# draw player
pygame.draw.circle(screen, red, [x, y], 6)
```

5. Below it add this code to draw the ball:

```
# draw ball
pygame.draw.circle(screen, blue, [ballX, ballY], 6)
```

6. Save the program and run it using Run⇨Run Module. You should see a blue dot appear in the window. (Trying moving the red player over it. You'll find that nothing happens—yet!) Close the game window and run it again. The ball should now be in a new random position (see Figure 6-6).

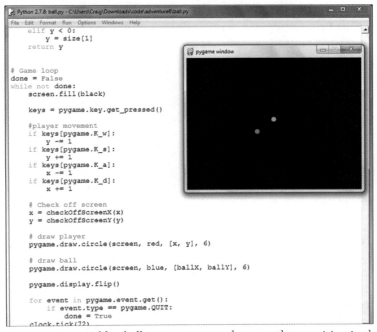

FIGURE 6-6 A blue ball is now generated at a random position in the game.

Creating Collisions

At the moment, when your player kicks the ball it doesn't do anything. To fix this you're going to add some code that checks whether the player is near the ball and causes a small explosion if they are:

1. In the `movementGame.py` program find the `checkOffScreenY()` function. Below that function add this function that will check if the player is touching the ball:

```python
def checkTouching():
    """Causes a mini explosion if the players are touching"""
    global x
    global ballX
    global y
    global ballY

    # Check if player and ball are touching
    if -10 < y - ballY < 10 and -10 < x - ballX < 10:
        #draw an explosion
        pygame.draw.circle(screen, white, [x, y], 15)

        xDiff = x - ballX
        yDiff = y - ballY

        # check if ball is on edge of screen
        if ballX == 0:
            xDiff -= 5
        elif ballX == size[0]:
            xDiff += 5
        if ballY == 0:
            yDiff -= 5
        elif ballY == size[1]:
            yDiff += 5

        # move the ball and player
        x += xDiff * 3
        ballX -= xDiff * 3

        y += yDiff * 3
        ballY -= yDiff * 3
```

2. Next, find this code in the program:

```python
# draw player
pygame.draw.circle(screen, red, [x, y], 6)
```

3. Above it add this code to check if the player is touching the ball:

```python
# Check if player is touching the ball
checkTouching()
```

4. Save the program and test it. Brilliant! Whenever the player kicks the ball there's a small explosion and the player and ball move in opposite directions (see Figure 6-7).

FIGURE 6-7 When the player collides with the ball there is a small explosion.

You may notice that if you kick the ball to the side of the screen gets stuck. To fix this, you can use the functions on the ball's position variables to check whether the player is offscreen. Let's do this now:

1. Find this code in your program:

```
# Check off screen
x = checkOffScreenX(x)
y = checkOffScreenY(y)
```

2. Directly beneath it add this code to check whether the ball is offscreen:

```
ballX = checkOffScreenX(ballX)
ballY = checkOffScreenY(ballY)
```

DIGGING INTO THE CODE

The `global` keyword allows your function to change the value of a variable that is created outside of the function. If you didn't include the `global` variable, the program would display an error message when you try to change the value of the `x`, `y`, `ballX` and `ballY` variables.

To check if the ball and the player are touching, the program uses something called a range check. A range check uses two `less than` operators to check if one value is between another two. For example, `-5 < y - ballY < 5` checks if the distance between the ball and the player is between -5 and 5. So that the `x` and `y` variables for the ball are checked at the same time, an `and` operator is used to combine two range checks.

There's a bug with this code when the ball is on the edge of the screen, and the `if` statements in this part of the program are the first part of the code that will fix this. You'll return to the second part in a second.

3. Save the program and run it. Now your player can kick the ball off the side of the screen and it will reappear on the opposite side.

Goal!

Now that the player can kick the ball around the screen, you're going to add a goal to the game so that the player has something to kick it at and score points. The program will draw a goal at the center of the screen and check whether the player has kicked the ball into the goal. Figure 6-8 shows what the goal will look like.

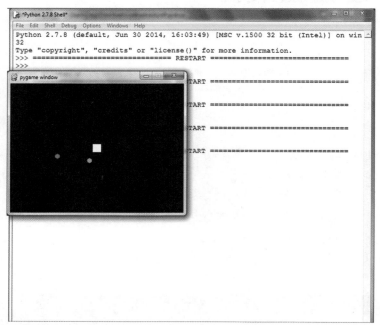

FIGURE 6-8 The goal

1. In the program, find the ball position lines of code that look like this:

```
# ball position
ballX = random.randrange(0, size[0])
ballY = random.randrange(0, size[1])
```

Like the code that checks whether the player and the ball are touching, this part of the program uses two range checks to check whether the ball is in the goal. The code that does this is: `goalX <= ballX <= goalX + goalH and goalY <= ballY <= goalY + goalH`. If the ball is in the goal the points are increased by 1 and the ball is reset at a new random position.

2. Below that, add this code to set the position and size of the goal and set the points to 0:

```
# Goal position
goalX = size[0] / 2 - 10
goalY = size[1] / 2 - 10
goalW = 20
goalH = 20

# points
points = 0
```

3. Next, find this line in the game loop:

```
screen.fill(black)
```

4. Below that, add this code to draw the goal:

```
#Draw the goal
pygame.draw.rect(screen, white, (goalX, goalY, goalW, ↵
          goalH))
```

5. Below that, add this code to check the ball is in the goal:

```
# Check ball is in goal
if goalX <= ballX <= goalX + goalH and goalY <= ballY ↵
        <= goalY + goalH:
    points += 1
    ballX = random.randrange(0, size[0])
    ballY = random.randrange(0, size[0])
```

6. Now save the program and run it. You should be able to make your player kick the ball into the goal. The ball resets and teleports to a new random position every time you do this.

Fantastic! You've created a program in which a player can score goals and score points. But how do you know how many points they've scored? Here's how to create a display for the points:

1. Below the code that checks the player is touching the ball, add the following code:

```
# Draw points
for point in range(points):
    pointX = 0 + point * 5
pygame.draw.rect(screen, white, (pointX, 3, 4, 7))
```

2. You also want your program to print the total points when the game ends. After the final line of the program, which should be `pygame.quit()`, add the following line of code:

```
print "Total points: " + str(points)
```

Save the program and run it. What happens? Whenever you score a goal, a small white line, one for each point, should appear in the top-left of the screen (see Figure 6-9). Finally, when you exit the window, your total points will be printed to the Python shell (see Figure 6-10).

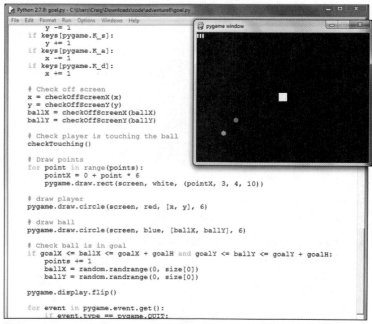

FIGURE 6-9 The points are displayed in the top-left corner of the screen.

DIGGING INTO THE CODE

This code uses a `for` loop to draw the points onto the screen. The `for` loop will repeat the code inside the body of the loop. Using the `range()` function means that it will repeat the same number of times as there are points. So if you have four points, the loop will repeat four times.

The points are displayed as small white rectangles in the top-left corner of the screen. The x position of the point is set every five pixels using the `pointX` variable. Using the `point` variable, the position of each point will increase on the x-axis when the loop repeats.

```
Python 2.7.8 Shell
File  Edit  Shell  Debug  Options  Windows  Help
Python 2.7.8 (default, Jun 30 2014, 16:03:49) [MSC v.1500 32 bit (Intel)] on win
32
Type "copyright", "credits" or "license()" for more information.
>>> ================================ RESTART ================================
>>>
Total points: 3
>>> |
```

FIGURE 6-10 The program closes after 60 seconds, and the points are displayed in the Python shell.

Adding a Time Limit

At the moment the game does everything it needs to. Not very challenging though, is it? And it goes on forever! Why not add excitement by adding a time limit?

1. In your program find this code:

```
# Game loop
done = False
```

2. Below the code add this code to get the time that your program starts:

```
# get current time
timeStart = pygame.time.get_ticks()
```

3. Next, find this code:

```
clock.tick(72)
```

4. Below it, add this code to check if the game has lasted 60 seconds. If it has, it will exit the loop:

```
# Check elapsed time
timeNow = pygame.time.get_ticks()
if timeNow - timeStart >= 60000:
    done = True
```

The frame rate of the game is set to 72 using the `clock.tick(72)` statement. What happens to the game if you change this number? What happens if you increase the number? What happens if you decrease it? What happens if you try a really big number?

DIGGING INTO THE CODE

In order to create a time limit for the game, the `timeStart = pygame.time. get_ticks()` part of the code gets the time when the game loop started. At the end of game loop the program then checks whether more than 60000 milliseconds have passed (60000 milliseconds is the same as 60 seconds). If the game has been running for 60 seconds, the program will change the `done` variable to `True`, making the game loop exit.

CHALLENGE

At the moment the program doesn't display how many seconds are left in the game. Can you work out how to add a timer to the game? Use similar code to the points code to display a countdown or the elapsed time.

Python Command Quick Reference Table

Command	Description
`pressed = pygame.key.get pressed()`	This function in `PyGame` is used to get all the keys that are being pressed. It returns a list containing all the keys that are pressed.
`pressed[pygame.K w]`	The keypresses in the `get pressed()` list can be accessed using `pygame.K w`. The key that you want to check should be the last letter of the `pygame.K_w`; for example, the t key would be `pygame.K_t`.
`global variable`	Global variables are used in functions so that a function can change the value of a variable that was created outside of the function.
`-5 < x < 5`	Range checks check whether one value is between two other values. If the value is between the other two numbers, it evaluates to `True`, otherwise it evaluates to `False`.

Achievement Unlocked: **Skilled creator of a game using** `PyGame` **and the keyboard.**

Next Adventure

Hooray! You've written your first game with PyGame. So far you've made images and animations in Adventure 5 and created a small game with PyGame in this one. You've done a wide range of things with your game: created a character that can be moved with the keyboard, added a ball they can move, included a points system and a whole lot more.

In the next adventure, you'll make several short programs that use the mouse to do some really cool things.

Adventure 7
Creative Ways to Use a Mouse with PyGame

THE MOUSE IS an extremely versatile tool. Mice are simple to use and make interaction with the computer via GUIs very straightforward.

In this adventure, you'll learn how to use the mouse with Python and PyGame. You'll learn how to check for mouse clicks and find the position of the mouse pointer. By building on these basic things, you'll create some cool programs including a moving target game, a mesh drawer and a trail that follows the mouse around the window.

The mouse position uses coordinates to determine its position like other PyGame programs. Values for the coordinates are most frequently represented by x and y variables. The top-left corner has the coordinates 0, 0, with these x and y values increasing as the mouse moves farther to the right and downwards.

Getting the Mouse Position

For a video that walks you through the steps of finding and displaying the current mouse position, visit the companion website at www.wiley.com/go/adventuresinpython. Click the Videos tab and select the appropriate file.

Let's dive into using the mouse with Python and PyGame.

This first program will get the current position of the mouse and display it. The program is meant to show you how to get the mouse position; it doesn't do much else.

In this program, you press the left button on the mouse in order to display the value of the mouse position. As you move the mouse around the PyGame window the value of the mouse position will change. When you click again in the window, the new value will be displayed.

To keep things simple, the program will print the mouse's position in the Python shell when the mouse is clicked.

1. First up, open IDLE and create a new file with File⟳New Window.

2. Now in the new window, save the program as mousePos.py in a new folder called Adventure 7.

3. Click in the file editor and enter these lines of code to set up the PyGame window:

```python
import pygame
pygame.init()

windowSize = [400, 300]
screen = pygame.display.set_mode(windowSize)
clock = pygame.time.Clock()
```

4. To check if any of the mouse buttons have been pressed and to display the position of the click, add this code:

```python
done = False
while not done:
    for event in pygame.event.get():
        if event.type == pygame.MOUSEBUTTONDOWN:
            pos = pygame.mouse.get_pos()
            print pos
```

5. Finally, so that the window can be closed, add this code:

```python
        if event.type == pygame.QUIT:
            done = True
pygame.quit()
```

6. Save the program and run it with Run⟳Run Module.

7. When the window appears move your mouse into the window and click the left button on the mouse. The position of the mouse will be printed in the Python shell (see Figure 7-1).

FIGURE 7-1 Looking at the Python shell, you can see where the mouse button has been clicked.

Making a Button

In Adventure 3, you learned how to make buttons with `Tkinter`. Unlike `Tkinter`, `PyGame` doesn't have an inbuilt way to create buttons easily because it is made to create games and other multimedia. However, with a small amount of code you can create an area in the `PyGame` window that works like a button.

You're going to create a program that will create a rectangle in the middle of the window. When you click on the rectangle it will change the colour of the window, but when you click elsewhere in the window it will do nothing.

You'll then build upon this code to create a game where you have to click on a moving target.

There are a couple of functions in the code that work with the mouse in this program. The bit of code that gets the mouse position is `pos = pygame.mouse.get_pos()`. This function gets the current position of the mouse inside the PyGame window. It returns a **tuple** of the `x` and `y` positions as integers. A tuple is like a list, but the values of items in the list cannot be changed once they are created. Tuples can also be created like lists, but instead of using square brackets [] they use regular brackets (). You will come across tuples throughout your adventures.

The other bit of code that is specific to the mouse is the `if` statement that says `if event.type == pygame.MOUSEBUTTONDOWN:`. Mouse clicks are events in PyGame, which is why this code is inside of the `event` `for` loop. This `if` statement checks whether the event type is a mouse click.

You can of course put the code that gets the mouse position outside of the `event` `for` loop and you'll see examples of this in later exercises in this adventure.

DEFINITIONS

A **tuple** is like a list. Like a list it holds a collection of items, which can be stored in a single variable. Unlike a list, the values in a tuple cannot be changed after it has been created. When defining a tuple all of the items in the tuple are enclosed in regular brackets () with commas to separate them.

You can see the finished program in Figure 7-2.

Time to get going.

1. Open IDLE and create a new window with File➪New Window.

2. Save the program as `button.py` in the `Adventure 7` folder.

3. Add these lines of code to the top of your program to set up the `PyGame` window:

```
import pygame
pygame.init()

windowSize = [400, 300]
screen = pygame.display.set_mode(windowSize)
clock = pygame.time.Clock()
```

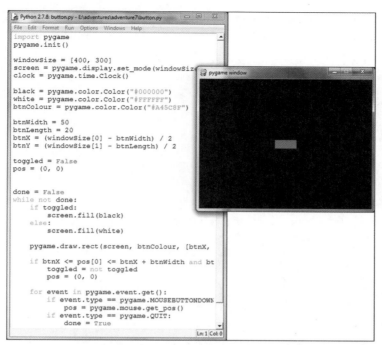

```
Python 2.7.8: button.py - E:\adventures\adventure7\button.py
File  Edit  Format  Run  Options  Windows  Help
import pygame
pygame.init()

windowSize = [400, 300]
screen = pygame.display.set_mode(windowSize
clock = pygame.time.Clock()

black = pygame.color.Color("#000000")
white = pygame.color.Color("#FFFFFF")
btnColour = pygame.color.Color("#A45C8F")

btnWidth = 50
btnLength = 20
btnX = (windowSize[0] - btnWidth) / 2
btnY = (windowSize[1] - btnLength) / 2

toggled = False
pos = (0, 0)


done = False
while not done:
    if toggled:
        screen.fill(black)
    else:
        screen.fill(white)

    pygame.draw.rect(screen, btnColour, [btnX,

    if btnX <= pos[0] <= btnX + btnWidth and bt
        toggled = not toggled
        pos = (0, 0)

    for event in pygame.event.get():
        if event.type == pygame.MOUSEBUTTONDOWN
            pos = pygame.mouse.get_pos()
        if event.type == pygame.QUIT:
            done = True
                                          Ln: 1 Col: 0
```

FIGURE 7-2 When the button in the middle of the screen is pressed, the background will change to black.

4. Next, add these lines to create three colours. The black and white colours are for the background and the `btnColour` colour variable is the colour for the button:

```
black = pygame.color.Color("#000000")
white = pygame.color.Color("#FFFFFF")
btnColour = pygame.color.Color("#A45C8F")
```

5. The next bit of the code sets the size and position of the rectangle for the button. It also sets the button toggled to `False` and the default position of the mouse. Add this code now:

```
btnWidth = 50
btnLength = 20
btnX = (windowSize[0] - btnWidth) / 2
btnY = (windowSize[1] - btnLength) / 2


toggled = False
pos = (0, 0)
```

6. The next bit of code starts the game loop. If the toggled variable is True, it will make the background colour of the window black, otherwise it will be white.

```
done = False
while not done:
    if toggled:
        screen.fill(black)
    else:
        screen.fill(white)
```

7. This code will draw the rectangle for the button and check if the button has been clicked. If it has been clicked, it will change the `toggled` variable, thereby changing the colour of the background:

```
pygame.draw.rect(screen, btnColour, [btnX, btnY, ↵
  btnWidth, btnLength])
if btnX <= pos[0] <= btnX + btnWidth and btnY <= ↵
  pos[1] <= btnY + btnLength:
    toggled = not toggled
    pos = [0, 0]
```

8. The final bit of code checks if the mouse button has been pressed and stores its position when it was clicked. It also checks if the window has been closed and updates the display:

```
for event in pygame.event.get():
    if event.type == pygame.MOUSEBUTTONDOWN:
        pos = pygame.mouse.get_pos()
    if event.type == pygame.QUIT:
        done = True
pygame.display.flip()
clock.tick(10)
pygame.quit()
```

9. Save the program and run it using Run⇨Run Module.

10. When the window opens, click on the button and the background colour will change. Clicking elsewhere on the window will not do anything.

Moving Target

For a video that walks you through the steps of creating a moving target, visit the companion website at www.wiley.com/go/adventuresinpython. Click the Videos tab and select the appropriate file.

Now that you can create a clickable area in the PyGame window, let's modify the code to turn it into a game.

DIGGING INTO THE CODE

The line of code `toggled = not toggled` makes the value of `toggled` the opposite of what it was. If it was `True` it will now be `False` and vice versa. Below this the `pos = (0, 0)` code resets the position of the mouse click to the corner of the screen. If this line of code weren't there, the screen would flash between black and white until you clicked somewhere else on the window background.

To check if the mouse position is inside the area of the button, a range check is used. A range check determines if one value is in between two other values. For example, the code `btnX <= pos[0] <= btnX + btnWidth` checks if the mouse's x position is greater than the button's left side and less than the button's right side. The code `btnY <= pos[1] <= btnY + btnLength` does the same with the y position of the mouse.

The code `btnX = (windowSize[0] - btnWidth) / 2` uses the button width and window size to calculate the x position of the button automatically. This means that the window size and button width can be changed and the button will stay in the centre of the screen.

In the game, the clickable area will move around the window randomly. When the player clicks the area they will get points, but the difficulty of the game will also increase, making the random movements of the button more erratic and therefore harder to click.

In Figure 7-3 you can see that the button you created in the last program will now move around the window.

1. This code builds upon the previous program, so open the previous program called `button.py` in the `Adventure 7` folder.

2. Save the program as `movingTarget.py` in the `Adventure 7` folder.

3. On the first line of the program, add this line to import the random module:

```
import random
```

4. Find these lines of code:

```
toggled = False
pos = (0, 0)
```

5. Below this, add this line of code to record the number of times the player has clicked the button:

```
points = 0
```

FIGURE 7-3 The more you click the target, the more erratically it will move.

6. Now find these lines of code:

```
if btnX <= pos[0] <= btnX + btnWidth and
   btnY <= pos[1] <= btnY + btnLength:
   toggled = not toggled
   pos = (0, 0)
```

7. Directly below that, add this code to increase the points awarded when the target is clicked and randomly move the position of the target:

```
points += 1

btnX += random.randint(-1 - points, 1 + points)
btnY += random.randint(-1 - points, 1 + points)
```

8. Finally, on the last line of the program add this statement so that the points are displayed in the Python shell after the window has been closed:

```
print points
```

9. Now save the program and run it using Run⇨Run Module.

10. When the window opens you can click on the target. It should start moving around. The more you click, the farther it will move.

At the moment, the target for the game is very basic. It is just a rectangle. But with a few extra lines of code you can create your own image for the target. Try turning it into a monster or a robot.

Another challenge that you could add is to stop the rectangle from leaving the window. At the moment it will sometimes disappear off the edge of the window. Can you work out how to stop it from leaving the window?

In 2D computer games, rectangles are used to detect whether an enemy has been hit. This is known as a *hit box*. This is very similar to the button and moving target programs you've just made, although in computer games the hit box is usually invisible.

A **hit box** is used in video games when checking if a player, enemy, object or terrain are touching. They are usually rectangular in shape and surround the object representing the edges of where the game object will start to come into contact with other objects.

Exploding Clicks

With some minor modifications to the program you can make quite a drastic change to its effects. In this program, you'll create an explosion effect that will appear every time you click in the window.

The colour of the explosions will be randomised every time you click the mouse.

1. Open IDLE and create a new file with File➪New Window.

2. Save the program as `explosions.py` in the `Adventure 7` folder.

3. First add the following lines to the program:

```
import pygame
import random
pygame.init()
```

4. The next bit of code is a function that will generate a random colour, and it will be used later in the program. Add it below the code you've already written:

```python
def randColour():
    r = random.randint(0, 255)
    g = random.randint(0, 255)
    b = random.randint(0, 255)
    return (r, g, b)
```

5. The next bit of code will set up the window and create the colours for the background and default value of the explosion. The other variables record the number of frames that the explosion animation will use and the maximum number of frames in the animation:

```python
windowSize = [400, 300]
screen = pygame.display.set_mode(windowSize)
clock = pygame.time.Clock()

black = pygame.color.Color("#000000")
colour = randColour()

count = 0
click = False
limit = 30
pos = (0, 0)
```

6. The next bit creates the game loop and draws the explosion to the screen:

```python
done = False
while not done:
    screen.fill(black)

    if click and count < limit:
        pygame.draw.circle(screen, colour, pos, count)
        count += 1
        if count >= limit:
            click = False
```

7. The final bit of the program gets the position of mouse clicks and allows the window to be closed:

```python
    for event in pygame.event.get():
        if event.type == pygame.MOUSEBUTTONDOWN:
            pos = pygame.mouse.get_pos()
            click = True
            count = 0
            colour = randColour()
        if event.type == pygame.QUIT:
            done = True
    pygame.display.flip()
    clock.tick(60)
pygame.quit()
```

8. Save the program and run it using Run⇨Run Module.

9. When the window opens, click anywhere in the window. See what happens? A randomly coloured explosion appears where you clicked the mouse. You can see an example of this in Figure 7-4.

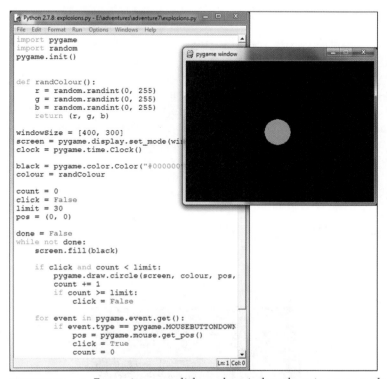

FIGURE 7-4 Every time you click on the window there is a new explosion.

DIGGING INTO THE CODE

The size of the circle for the explosion will increase every time the loop repeats until its radius is 30. To do this, the `count` variable sets the size of the circle and increases by 1 every time the loop repeats. The `limit` variable sets the maximum size of the circle. Increasing the value of this variable will make the explosion bigger and grow for a longer amount of time, and reducing the value will make the explosion smaller and end in a shorter amount of time.

Making a Mesh

VIDEO

For a video that walks you through the steps of creating a 3D mesh, visit the companion website at www.wiley.com/go/adventuresinpython. Click the Videos tab and select the appropriate file.

Flexibility is one of benefits of using PyGame with Python. So far in this adventure, you've seen several variations on programs that use the mouse position and mouse clicks.

The next program will show you how flexible PyGame and Python can be. The program will allow you to draw lines that look like a 3D mesh. A 3D mesh is a collection of joined lines that are used to make 3D models. This program will create something that looks like a 3D mesh but doesn't work like one—it just looks similar.

You can see an example of this program in Figure 7-5.

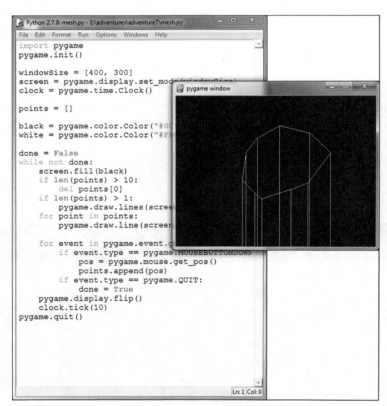

FIGURE 7-5 Clicking anywhere on the window adds a new point to the mesh.

When you click on the window the program will create a new point in the mesh. Every following click will create a new point in the mesh. The program will limit the number of points in the mesh to 10 points, after which it will delete the oldest point and update the mesh.

1. Open IDLE and create a new file with File⇨New Window.

2. Save the program as mesh.py in the Adventure 7 folder.

3. In the new file add these lines of code:

```
import pygame
pygame.init()

windowSize = [400, 300]
screen = pygame.display.set_mode(windowSize)
clock = pygame.time.Clock()
```

4. The next bit of the code is a list that will record every position that has been clicked with the mouse. It will be used later in the program to draw the lines for the mesh:

```
points = []
```

5. Add this code, which creates the colours and starts the game loop:

```
black = pygame.color.Color("#000000")
white = pygame.color.Color("#FFFFFF")

done = False
while not done:
    screen.fill(black)
```

6. Next, the program will check if there are 10 points in the mesh. If there are it will remove the first point in the mesh. The second bit will draw all of the points in the mesh:

```
    if len(points) > 10:
        del points[0]
    if len(points) > 1:
        pygame.draw.lines(screen, white, True, points)
```

7. The next bit of the code will link each point in the mesh with the bottom of the window by creating straight lines. Add this code to the program:

```
    for point in points:
        pygame.draw.line(screen, white, point, [point[0],
                         windowSize[1]])
```

8. The last bit of code checks for mouse clicks and allows the window to be closed:

```
for event in pygame.event.get():
    if event.type == pygame.MOUSEBUTTONDOWN:
        pos = pygame.mouse.get_pos()
        points.append(pos)
    if event.type == pygame.QUIT:
        done = True
    pygame.display.flip()
    clock.tick(10)
pygame.quit()
```

9. Save the program and run it with Run➪Run Module.

10. Now when the window opens you can click anywhere in the window and a line will appear that joins the point where you clicked to the bottom of the window. Clicking again will create a second point that joins to the first. The more you click, the more lines will appear. You can create 10 lines in total.

What happens if you change the value 10 in this statement? `if len(points) > 10:`

What happens if you increase or decrease the value? Can you change the code so there are no limits to the number of lines you create?

DIGGING INTO THE CODE

The positions that you click on the window are stored as a list in the `points` variable. Every time the mouse is clicked the `points.append(pos)` adds the new position to the end of the list. The PyGame `lines()` function draws a set of lines. The function takes the points list as an argument to determine where it will draw the lines.

The `True` argument in the `points()` function means that the lines will be closed to create a polygon. In other words, the last point in the list will connect to the first point, closing the lines. Changing this value to `False` will mean that this line will not be drawn.

In the program, the item at index position 0 in the points list is deleted if the number of items in the list is greater than 10. When this happens, all of the other items in the list are moved forward a position. The second item in index 1 moves into the index 0, index 2 moves to index 1, index 3 to index 2 and so on.

Creating Mouse Trails

For a video that walks you through the steps of creating mouse trails, visit the companion website at www.wiley.com/go/adventuresinpython. Click the Videos tab and select the appropriate file.

This final program in this adventure creates a trail of lines behind the mouse. The difference between this program and the others in the adventure is that it doesn't use mouse clicks, just the position of the mouse. The mouse trails program not only looks cool, it also shows you how you can follow the mouse's position without needing to click any buttons.

Look at Figure 7-6 to see the trails following the mouse.

1. Open IDLE and create a new file with File⇨New Window.

2. Save the new file as `mouseTrails.py` in the `Adventure 7` folder.

3. The next part of the program sets up the PyGame window, creates a list for the points of the trail that will be stored and also creates two variables that store colours:

```
import pygame
pygame.init()

windowSize = [400, 300]
screen = pygame.display.set_mode(windowSize)
clock = pygame.time.Clock()

points = []

white = pygame.color.Color("#FFFFFF")
black = pygame.color.Color("#000000")
```

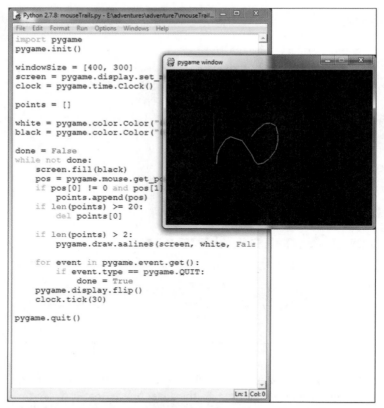

FIGURE 7-6 The trails follow the mouse all over the window.

4. The next bit of the code starts the game loop and gets the position of the mouse at the start of the loop. Add it to your program now:

```python
done = False
while not done:
    screen.fill(black)
    pos = pygame.mouse.get_pos()
```

5. When the window opens, the mouse will have a position of (0, 0). This code stops the program drawing a line from this position. It also limits the number of points to 20:

```python
    if pos[0] != 0 and pos[1] != 0:
        points.append(pos)
    if len(points) >= 20:
        del points[0]
```

6. In order for lines to be drawn properly, there need to be at least two points in the list. This code checks for this and then draws all of the points to create a trail behind the mouse:

```
    if len(points) >= 2:
pygame.draw.aalines(screen, white, False, points)
```

7. The final bit of the code allows the window of the program to be closed:

```
    for event in pygame.event.get():
        if event.type == pygame.QUIT:
            done = True
    pygame.display.flip()
    clock.tick(30)

pygame.quit()
```

8. Now run the program with Run⇨Run Module.

9. When the window opens, move the mouse around. It will magically be followed by a trail of lines.

DIGGING INTO THE CODE

To draw the lines in this program, the aalines() function is used. This is almost the same as the lines() function that you used in the previous program. The difference with the aalines() function is that it draws **anti-aliased lines**. Anti-aliasing means that extra pixels are added to the lines so that they look smoother. Compare the lines in this program with those in the previous program to see the difference.

The other difference in this program is that the argument that closes the lines is False. This means that the first and last lines are not connected so that it looks like a single trail is following the mouse.

An **anti-aliased line** has extra pixels added to make it look smoother. Lines without anti-aliasing are just made up of solid pixels and they can look jagged and unsmooth. To make lines look smoother, anti-aliasing adds extra semi-transparent pixels to the lines at certain points and also to the line corners. You can see the difference between lines with and without anti-aliasing in Figure 7-7.

FIGURE 7-7 Lines with and without anti-aliasing. Notice the extra pixels on the line with anti-aliasing.

WHAT HAPPENS?

What happens if you change the anti-aliased lines to lines without anti-aliasing? Can you see the difference between the two?

Python Command Quick Reference Table

Command	Description
`if event.type == pygame.MOUSEBUTTONDOWN:`	When any mouse button is pressed, a `PyGame MOUSEBUTTONDOWN` event is created. To get this event, this code is used.
`pygame.mouse.get_pos()`	This function finds the position of the mouse and returns the x and y values as a tuple.
`1 < x < 5`	A range check is used to check if one value is between two others. If it is, it will evaluate to `True`; if it is not, it will evaluate to `False`.
`len(list)`	To check the number of items in a list (and any other collections, such as tuples), the `list` variable is used as an argument in the `len()` function.
`list.append()`	To add an item to the end of a list, the `append()` function is used. The value to be added to the list is included as an argument.
`del list[index]`	To delete an item from a list, the `del` operator is used. The item of the list is accessed using its index position, and the `del` operator goes before it.
`pygame.draw.lines()`	The `PyGame lines()` function will draw a series of lines. The function takes four arguments: the surface it will be drawn to; its colour; whether the lines are closed to create a polygon; and a list of the points that the lines will be drawn.
`pygame.draw.aalines`	The `aalines()` function creates a set of lines like the `lines()` function, but will make the lines look smooth.

Achievement Unlocked: Skilled manipulator of the mouse to create superb programs with PyGame.

Next Adventure

Good work! In this adventure you've learned how to use the mouse with Python and PyGame. You've created a number of fun programs including a moving target game, a mesh drawer and a trail of lines that follows the mouse.

In the next adventure, you'll learn how to use images with Python and PyGame. You'll find out how to load images into your programs, amongst other things. By the end of the adventure, you'll be using images and the keyboard to move a character around the game window.

Adventure 8
Using Images
with PyGame

IN THIS ADVENTURE, you'll learn how to use images with Python and `PyGame`. During previous adventures you've used `PyGame`'s drawing functions to draw shapes. You've discovered how flexible this is and how much it allows you to do, but it can't do everything! Sometimes you will want to use images from other programs instead of drawing them with code.

During this adventure, you'll create programs to load and layer images. You'll create a program that lets you add a moustache to any image and another program to move a sprite around the window, which forms the basis of a game.

Loading an Image

For a video that walks you through the steps of loading images, visit the companion website at www.wiley.com/go/adventuresinpython. Click the Videos tab and select the appropriate file.

The first thing you'll do in this adventure is learn how to load and display an image. Before you can start, you'll need to save your chosen images into the folder that the program will be saved in. In this adventure I've chosen the images for you. To download these images, follow the steps given in the Appendix.

Finished? Once you have the images, copy all of them into the Adventure 8 folder.

The first images you will be using are catSmall.png, catLarge.png, hat.png and space.png. Make sure they are in the Adventure 8 folder; if they aren't then make sure you follow the steps in the Appendix. If they are in the correct place then you may begin.

This program will display a picture of a cat. The program loads an image into Python using PyGame and displays it in a new window.

1. Open IDLE and create a new file with File⇨New Window.

2. Save the program as loadImage.py in the Adventure 8 folder.

3. In the file editor, add the following code to set up the PyGame window:

```
import pygame
pygame.init()

windowSize = [400, 300]
screen = pygame.display.set_mode(windowSize)
```

4. Next, the image is loaded into the program using the load() function and placed onto the window using the blit() function. Add this code to your program now:

```
image = pygame.image.load('catLarge.png')
screen.blit(image, (0, 0))
```

5. Finally add this code so that the window can be closed:

```
done = False
while not done:
    for event in pygame.event.get():
        if event.type == pygame.QUIT:
            done = True
    pygame.display.flip()

pygame.quit()
```

6. Save the program and run it using Run⇨Run Module.

7. When the window opens you should see a picture of a cat in the top-left corner of the window, as in Figure 8-1.

TIPS & TRICKS

The cat has a transparent background so that you can see the window's black background around the image. This has a number of benefits. If the area around the cat's head in the image weren't transparent there would be a rectangle around the image. This wouldn't look good. The transparency means if you choose to change the colour of the background later, you won't have to change the cat's image to match. It also means that, if you want to put another image behind the cat, you will be able to see it.

FIGURE 8-1 The image loads into the window. You can see the black background due to transparency around the image of the cat.

Cat © Jagodka/Shutterstock.com

DIGGING INTO THE CODE

You use the `image.load()` function to load images into the program. The name of the image you want your program to load should be placed as an argument in the function. In this program, the image is stored in the same folder as the program. You can load as many images as you want in a single program. The main image formats that `PyGame` can use are .png, .jpg, .gif and .bmp; the programs can use other image formats too, but these are less common.

In order for the image to be displayed, the image needs to be placed onto the `PyGame` window surface. To place the image onto a surface, you use the `blit()` function. **Blitting** places the image at the location specified in the argument. In this example, the image is blitted onto co-ordinates (0, 0).

Blit is the process of combining two images together by placing one on top of another. The pixels of one image are placed on top of another to create a new image. This is like layering images on top of one another and is used to place images on top of backgrounds.

Layering Images

For a video that walks you through the steps of layering images, visit the companion website at www.wiley.com/go/adventuresinpython. Click the Videos tab and select the appropriate file.

You're now going to give your cat a hat. To do this, you need a program that uses two images, one of a cat and the other of a hat, which are loaded from files. The cat's face is placed on the background of the window, and the hat is placed on top of it. The position of the hat is set in the program. This program shows you how to layer images on top of each other.

Time to get started:

1. Make sure that IDLE is open and create a new file with File⇨New Window.

2. Save the program as `layeredImage.py` in the `Adventure 8` folder.

3. In the file editor add this code to set up the `PyGame` window:

```
import pygame
pygame.init()

windowSize = [400, 300]
screen = pygame.display.set_mode(windowSize)
```

4. Next, the two images are loaded. Add this code now:

```
cat = pygame.image.load('catLarge.png')
hat = pygame.image.load('hat.png')
```

5. The next bit of code places the images onto the screen surface. As the hat image is blitted second, it will appear on top:

```
x = 0
y = 0

screen.blit(cat, (x + 10, y + 50))
screen.blit(hat, (x + 7, y))
```

6. The last part of the code allows the window to be closed:

```
done = False
while not done:
    for event in pygame.event.get():
        if event.type == pygame.QUIT:
            done = True
    pygame.display.flip()

pygame.quit()
```

7. Save the program and run it using Run⇨Run Module.

8. Load the program. The cat should now be sporting a smart bowler hat (see Figure 8-2).

FIGURE 8-2 The cat is now wearing a hat. The image has a transparent background so that you can see the cat's face.

Cat © Jagodka/Shutterstock.com

Hat © Mayboroda/Shutterstock.com

Getting the two images lined up in the correct location is very important for this program. The position of the images is set in the second argument of the blit() function. If you create your own programs, you can adjust the position of the images by changing the values in the second argument.

Randomly Layering Images

There is no limit to the number of images you can blit to the PyGame window surface. Images will stay on the surface, meaning that you can blit images on top of each other.

The images will stay on the surface until you fill the surface with a colour or place another image over the top of it—you'll cover that later in this adventure.

Next, you're going to layer images randomly all over the window surface. The end result should look something like Figure 8-3. The images layer on top of each other because you never refresh the background and, just to maximize the randomness, you're going to rotate each image by a random angle.

FIGURE 8-3 The image of the cat appears randomly all over the window.

Cat © Jagodka/Shutterstock.com

1. Open IDLE and create a new file with File➪New Window.

2. Save the program as `randomImages.py` in the `Adventure` 8 folder.

3. In the file, add the following code to set up the `PyGame` window:

```python
import random
import pygame
pygame.init()

windowSize = [400, 300]
screen = pygame.display.set_mode(windowSize)
clock = pygame.time.Clock()
```

4. Next, the program loads the image you've chosen for the background and the image you've chosen to be repeated on top of it. The background is then blitted onto the background. Add this code:

```python
image = pygame.image.load('catSmall.png')
bg = pygame.image.load('space.png')

screen.blit(bg, (0, 0))
```

5. Now the program starts the game loop. In the loop, it generates a random location for the image and rotates it by a random angle:

```python
done = False
while not done:
    x = random.randint(0, windowSize[0])
    y = random.randint(0, windowSize[1])
    angle = random.randint(0, 360)
    rotatedImage = pygame.transform.rotate(image, angle)
    screen.blit(rotatedImage, (x, y))
```

6. Finally, the program uses this code so that the window can be closed:

```python
    for event in pygame.event.get():
        if event.type == pygame.QUIT:
            done = True
    pygame.display.flip()
    clock.tick(10)

pygame.quit()
```

7. Save the program and run it using Run➪Run Module.

8. When the window opens, pictures of cats should appear randomly appear all over the window on top of a background picture of space.

Adding a Moustache to a Photograph

VIDEO

For a video that walks you through the steps of adding this moustache, visit the companion website at www.wiley.com/go/adventuresinpython. Click the Videos tab and select the appropriate file.

You can create some really cool programs by using images and the mouse. You're now going to use the mouse to put a moustache on the cat's face, as in Figure 8-4. This program combines code from the programs you've already created in this adventure and in Adventure 7 when you learned how to use a mouse with PyGame. Why not try using a picture of your own instead of the cat image?

Time to get started:

1. Open IDLE and create a new window with File⇨New Window.

2. Save the program as `moustache.py` in the `Adventure 8` folder.

3. Add this code to set up the PyGame window:

```
import pygame
pygame.init()

windowSize = [400, 300]
screen = pygame.display.set_mode(windowSize)
```

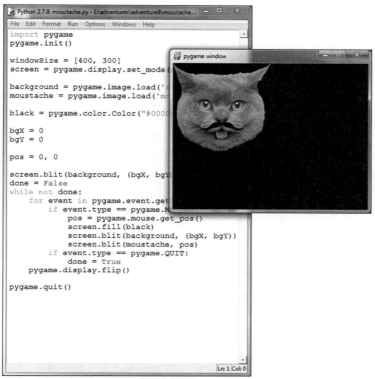

FIGURE 8-4 The cat now has a moustache.

Cat © Jagodka/Shutterstock.com

4. Next, you're going to load the face and moustache images. Alongside this, the colour black is created and the background image placed onto the window:

```
background = pygame.image.load('catLarge.png')
moustache = pygame.image.load('moustache.png')

black = pygame.color.Color("#000000")

bgPos = (0, 0)
pos = (0, 0)
screen.blit(background, bgPos)
```

5. Next, the game loop is started:

```
done = False
while not done:
```

6. The `event for` loop checks if the mouse has been clicked. If it has, it will refresh the window's background and place the moustache image where the mouse was clicked. Add this code now:

```
for event in pygame.event.get():
    if event.type == pygame.MOUSEBUTTONDOWN:
        pos = pygame.mouse.get_pos()
        screen.fill(black)
        screen.blit(background, bgPos)
        screen.blit(moustache, pos)
```

7. Finally, add this code so that the window can be closed:

```
    if event.type == pygame.QUIT:
        done = True
    pygame.display.flip()
pygame.quit()
```

8. Save the program and run it using Run↪Run Module.

9. When the window opens, the picture of the cat will be in the background. Here's where the fun starts: you can now click the mouse anywhere in the window and a moustache will miraculously appear at that point.

DIGGING INTO THE CODE

In this program, clicking will create a new moustache at a new location. So that the window updates and doesn't display the old moustache at the same time, the program fills the background with black and redraws the background. If the program didn't do this, the old moustache images would stay displayed on the screen.

CHALLENGE

There are a number of ways you could change the program. Try using your own images instead of the ones provided. Use a picture of yourself to add a moustache to your face. Change the moustache to something else, like a hat.

Making Sprites

For a video that walks you through the steps of making sprites, visit the companion website at www.wiley.com/go/adventuresinpython. Click the Videos tab and select the appropriate file.

In 2D computer games, the player and other characters in the game often have collections of images for all their movement and actions. These are called **sprites**. When combined in animations, the collection of images make the sprite look like it's moving. In this part of the adventure, you'll learn how to make basic sprite animations using images in PyGame.

A **sprite** is a collection of images that is used to represent a character in games. Sprites include all of the images for the animations of a character that will be displayed in a game.

There are several ways to use sprites in PyGame. PyGame even has prebuilt methods for managing sprites, such as creating groups of sprites and checking if sprites are touching. You won't explore sprites in much depth in this adventure, but will focus on using images to create movement animations.

In these programs, you will use the image functions that you've already learned in this adventure to make animations for sprite movement.

The first program will allow the sprite to move in one direction. You'll then build on top of that to allow it to move in all directions. Finally, you'll add an awesome teleportation animation.

Creating a Walking Animation

Let's get going on the first part of the program, in which you create a sprite that can walk down the window when the s key is pressed (see Figure 8-5). Animations are a necessary part of games. They help the players understand what is going on in the game and make the game more interactive than just using single images. For example, walking animations help make player movement look more relatable to players.

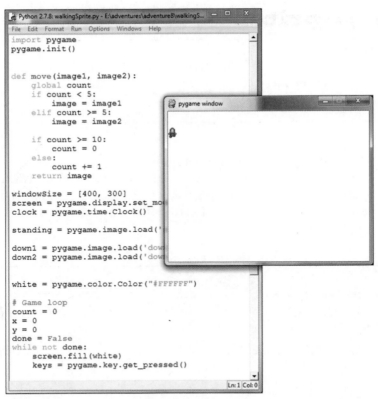

FIGURE 8-5 You can make the sprite walk down the window by using the s key.

The sprite you will be using in this program is an adventurer with a hat and a beard. The sprite is similar in size to some classic modern adventure games. With the knowledge you gain in this chapter and later chapters, you could develop this program or even further to turn it into a full game.

1. Open IDLE and create a new file with File↪New Window.

2. Save the program as `walkingSprite.py` in the `Adventure 8` folder.

3. In the file editor, copy these lines of code so that your program can use PyGame:

```python
import pygame
pygame.init()
```

4. The next bit of code is a function that chooses which picture to use for the current frame of the walking animation. Two images are used here for the walking animation so that the program makes it look like the player is walking when they move. To do this, it uses the count variable and, depending on its value, it returns one of the two images in the animation:

```
def move(image1, image2):
    global count
    if count < 5:
        image = image1
    elif count >= 5:
        image = image2

    if count >= 10:
        count = 0
    else:
        count += 1
    return image
```

5. The next bit of code sets up the PyGame window. Add it to the file editor:

```
windowSize = [400, 300]
screen = pygame.display.set_mode(windowSize)
clock = pygame.time.Clock()
```

6. The next part of the code loads the images for the standing and downward movement animation. It also creates the colour for the background. Add it to your program now:

```
standing = pygame.image.load('standing.png')

down1 = pygame.image.load('down1.png')
down2 = pygame.image.load('down2.png')

white = pygame.color.Color("#FFFFFF")
```

7. The next part of the program adds the count, x and y variables. The count variable is used in the animations for timing the changes between images. As usual, the x and y variables are used to record the position of the sprite:

```
count = 0
x = 0
y = 0
```

8. The next part of the program starts the game loop and checks if any keys have been pressed:

```
done = False
while not done:
    screen.fill(white)
    keys = pygame.key.get_pressed()
```

9. The program then checks if the s key has been pressed and chooses the image to use for the animation with the `move()` function:

```
#player movement
if keys[pygame.K_s]:
    image = move(down1, down2)
    y += 1
```

10. If the key isn't pressed, the character will use the standing still image:

```
else:
    image = standing
```

11. Next, the program blits the image onto the screen surface at the x and y positions and allows the window to be closed:

```
screen.blit(image, (x, y))

for event in pygame.event.get():
    if event.type == pygame.QUIT:
        done = True

pygame.display.flip()
clock.tick(32)
pygame.quit()
```

12. Save the program and run it using Run⇨Run Module.

13. When the window opens, press the s key. Et voila! The sprite will start walking down the window.

DIGGING INTO THE CODE

The move() function that is created in this program takes two arguments, one for each of the images in the movement animation. The reason this is written as a function is so that you can reuse it for four different directions of movement, which you will add in the full program later in this adventure.

Walking in All Directions

Next it's time to expand your program. In the previous part, you made it so that the sprite could walk downwards. In this part you'll add code so that the sprite can walk in all directions (see Figure 8-6).

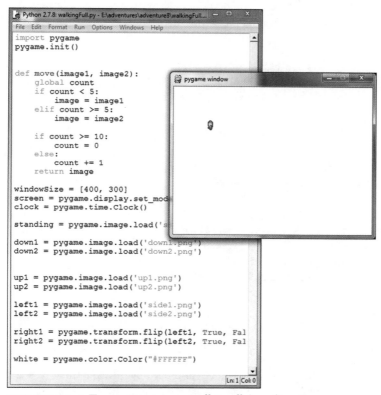

FIGURE 8-6 The sprite can now walk in all four directions.

1. Open the previous exercise in IDLE. You should have saved it as `walkingSprite.py`.

2. In the program, find these lines of code:

   ```
   down1 = pygame.image.load('down1.png')
   down2 = pygame.image.load('down2.png')
   ```

3. Underneath the code, add these lines to load the images for the other movement directions:

   ```
   up1 = pygame.image.load('up1.png')
   up2 = pygame.image.load('up2.png')
   ```

```
left1 = pygame.image.load('side1.png')
left2 = pygame.image.load('side2.png')

right1 = pygame.transform.flip(left1, True, False)
right2 = pygame.transform.flip(left2, True, False)
```

4. Next, find the `if` statement that looks like this:

```
if keys[pygame.K_s]:
    image = move(down1, down2)
    y += 1
else:
    image = standing
```

5. Change it to look like this, by adding the `elif` statements shown in bold here:

```
if keys[pygame.K_s]:
    image = move(down1, down2)
    y += 1
elif keys[pygame.K_w]:
    image = move(up1, up2)
    y -= 1
elif keys[pygame.K_a]:
    image = move(left1, left2)
    x -= 1
elif keys[pygame.K_d]:
    image = move(right1, right2)
    x += 1
else:
    image = standing
```

6. Save the program and run it using Run ⇨ Run Module.

7. You can now move the sprite up, down, left and right by pressing the w, a, s and d keys.

What happens when you press two keys at the same time? For example, press the w and a keys at the same time. Do you think the player will move diagonally or just up, down, left or right?

You might have found out that the player will not move diagonally. The order that the keys are in the `if` statement affects which direction they move when the keys are pressed. Can you work out how to change this so that the player can move diagonally? Hint: You made a similar program in Adventure 6 that allowed the player to move diagonally.

DIGGING INTO THE CODE

To save time, this program uses the same images for the left and right walking animations. The program loads the left-facing images and then flips them to display the images to face right. This is the code that does this: `right1 = pygame.transform.flip(left1, True, False)`. There is another line of code below this one that does the same for the second frame of the walking animation.

The Boolean arguments `True` and `False` in the `flip()` function determine whether the image will be flipped horizontally and/or vertically. The first of these two arguments flips the image horizontally (left to right) if it is `True`, and the second of these two arguments flips the image vertically (top to bottom) if it is `True`. This code flips the image horizontally, but not vertically, as the first of these two arguments is `True` and the second one is `False`.

CHALLENGE

The standing animation always faces downwards. Can you work out how to change it to face the same direction that the player just moved?

Teleportation

To finish off this program, you're now going to add a final animation that teleports your sprite to a new location when you press the space bar, as in Figure 8-7. You might use this in a game when your player needs to quickly move from one location to another or steps on a portal.

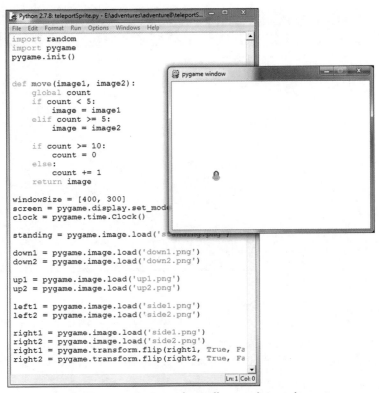

FIGURE 8-7 Pressing the space bar will now teleport the sprite to a random location.

To get this to work, the program will add an animation for the teleportation and set the coordinates of the sprite to a new random location. While this happens, movement with the keyboard will be locked so that no unexpected bugs can occur.

1. Make sure you have the `walkingSprite.py` file open in IDLE.

2. On the first line, add this code so that the program can use the random module:

   ```
   import random
   ```

3. In the program, find these lines of code:

   ```
   right1 = pygame.transform.flip(right1, True, False)
   right2 = pygame.transform.flip(right2, True, False)
   ```

4. Below it, add these statements to load the teleport images:

   ```
   teleport1 = pygame.image.load('teleport1.png')
   teleport2 = pygame.image.load('teleport2.png')
   teleport3 = pygame.image.load('teleport3.png')
   ```

5. Next, you need to add a variable to lock the movement when the sprite is tele-porting. Find these lines of code:

```
count = 0
x = 0
y = 0
```

6. Add this variable below them:

```
locked = False
```

7. To add the space bar as the key that will teleport the player, find this code:

```
if keys[pygame.K_s]:
    image = move(down1, down2)
    y += 1
elif keys[pygame.K_w]:
    image = move(up1, up2)
    y -= 1
elif keys[pygame.K_a]:
    image = move(left1, left2)
    x -= 1
elif keys[pygame.K_d]:
    image = move(right1, right2)
    x += 1
else:
    image = standing
    count = 0
```

8. Add the bold code to enable the program to teleport the player when the space key is pressed:

```
if keys[pygame.K_s]:
    image = move(down1, down2)
    y += 1
elif keys[pygame.K_w]:
    image = move(up1, up2)
    y -= 1
elif keys[pygame.K_a]:
    image = move(left1, left2)
    x -= 1
elif keys[pygame.K_d]:
    image = move(right1, right2)
    x += 1
elif keys[pygame.K_SPACE]:
    locked = True
else:
    image = standing
    count = 0
```

9. Add an `if` statement to the code and indent it so that it won't run if the locked `if` statement is `True`. This will stop the players from moving with the direction keys while they are teleporting:

```
if not locked:
    #player movement
    if keys[pygame.K_s]:
        image = move(down1, down2)
        y += 1
    elif keys[pygame.K_w]:
        image = move(up1, up2)
        y -= 1
    elif keys[pygame.K_a]:
        image = move(left1, left2)
        x -= 1
    elif keys[pygame.K_d]:
        image = move(right1, right2)
        x += 1
    elif keys[pygame.K_SPACE]:
        locked = True
    else:
        image = standing
        count = 0
```

10. Below this, add an `else` statement that runs the teleport animation and teleports the player to a random location:

```
else:
    if count < 5:
        image = teleport1
    elif count < 10:
        image = teleport2
    elif count < 15:
        image = teleport3
    else:
        x = random.randrange(0, windowSize[0])
        y = random.randrange(0, windowSize[1])
        count = 0
        locked = False
    count += 1
```

11. Save the program and run it using Run⇨Run Module.

12. When the program opens, press the space bar and watch the sprite teleport to a random position. If you press the w, a, s or d key during the teleport animation, the player should not move as the controls will be locked. The green flash that appears over the player is part of the animation that looks like the player is teleporting.

Python Command Quick Reference Table

Command	Description
`pygame.image.load()`	This function is used by `PyGame` to load images into the program.
`screen.blit()`	Blit is used to place images onto a `PyGame` surface.
`pygame.transform.rotate()`	The `rotate()` function is used with images to rotate them.
`pygame.transform.flip()`	Like the `rotate()` function, the `flip()` function flips an image along the x- and/or y-axis.

DIGGING INTO THE CODE

The reason that the program locks the movement when the teleport runs is so that unwanted glitches don't happen. The program creates the lock when the teleport first starts and unlocks it when it's finished. While the lock is set to `True`, you will not be able to move the player by pressing the w, a, s and d keys. You can't press the space bar to teleport the player while it's already tele-porting, either. Only when the teleportation animation has ended will you be able to press these keys again.

Achievement Unlocked: Rising star of images in `PyGame`.

Next Adventure

Great work! You've learned how to use images with Python and `PyGame`. You can now place images in the `PyGame` window, layer them and move them around. You've also learned how to use images to make sprites and control them with the keyboard.

In the next adventure, you'll learn how to use sounds with Python and `PyGame` and add sounds and music to the sprite program you made here.

Adventure 9
Using Sounds and Music with PyGame

IN THIS ADVENTURE, you'll learn how to use sounds and music with Python and PyGame. PyGame makes sounds and music available, including a whole load of useful functions that make it straightforward to add them to your program.

You'll make a loop that plays sounds, sounds that play when you press the keys on the keyboard and a basic music player. On top of this, you'll improve the sprite walking program that you made in Adventure 8 by adding music and sounds to it.

Before you start, you'll need to download the sample sounds and music needed for this adventure. You can find out how to do this in the Appendix. Make sure you save the files in the Adventure 9 folder.

Let's get going.

Playing Sounds

For a video that walks you through the steps of playing sounds, visit the companion website at www.wiley.com/go/adventuresinpython. Click the Videos tab and select the appropriate file.

In this first program, you'll learn how to play sounds. The program you make here will form the basis of other programs that you create in the adventure. Sounds are very important in games. They're an excellent way of sharing information with users and setting tone, all with just some noises. For example, in many video games you can often hear certain enemies sneaking up on you or you can tell if you managed to hit an object with your sword based on the sound it makes.

The program is very straightforward (see Figure 9-1); all it does is play a single sound before closing.

FIGURE 9-1 The completed code. Sadly, I can't take a screen print of the noise it makes!

1. Open IDLE and create a new file by clicking File⇨New Window.

2. Save the program as `play.py` in the `Adventure 9` folder.

3. Next add these lines of code so that the program can use `PyGame`:

   ```
   import pygame
   pygame.init()
   ```

4. The next bit of code will load the sound and play it. The sound in this program is called `hit.wav`, which is the name of the sound file. Add it to your program now:

   ```
   sound = pygame.mixer.Sound('hit.wav')
   sound.play()
   ```

This program introduces several new functions that let you use sound with `PyGame` and Python. The first one that you came across in this program was `sound = pygame.mixer.Sound('hit.wav')`. This code loads a sound file and stores it in a variable. In the previous program, `hit.wav` is the name of the file, which is then stored in the `sound` variable.

Once the sound is loaded the program can play it using the `play()` function. This will play the sound, but the program may close if there isn't a delay before the end of the file. To make sure the file can play without the program closing, the `pygame.time.wait()` function is used in this program. To make the delay last for the exact duration of the sound, the `sound.get_length()` function is used. This function returns the length of the sound in seconds (which is converted to milliseconds), meaning that the delay in the program will stop the program from ending until the sound has played.

You may have also noticed that the program did not create a `PyGame` window when it ran. This is because `PyGame` does not need a window to play sounds, as there are no graphics or images involved.

5. If the program finished here it would close before the sound had the chance to play in full, so you need to include a statement to keep the program open for the duration of the sound. Include it in your program now:

```
pygame.time.wait(int(sound.get_length()) * 1000)
```

6. Save the program and run it with Run⇨Run Module.

7. When the program runs, it will play the sound but no `PyGame` window will open—this isn't needed for the sound to play.

Creating a Noise Loop

In `PyGame`, you can load several sounds at once. In this program (see Figure 9-2), you'll create a loop that plays sounds. Every fourth time the loop repeats it will play a different sound. By adapting the program, you can make music or drum loops.

1. Open IDLE and create a new file with File⇨New Window.

2. Save the program as `noiseLoop.py` in the `Adventure 9` folder.

3. First add these two statements to allow the program to use `PyGame`:

```
import pygame
pygame.init()
```

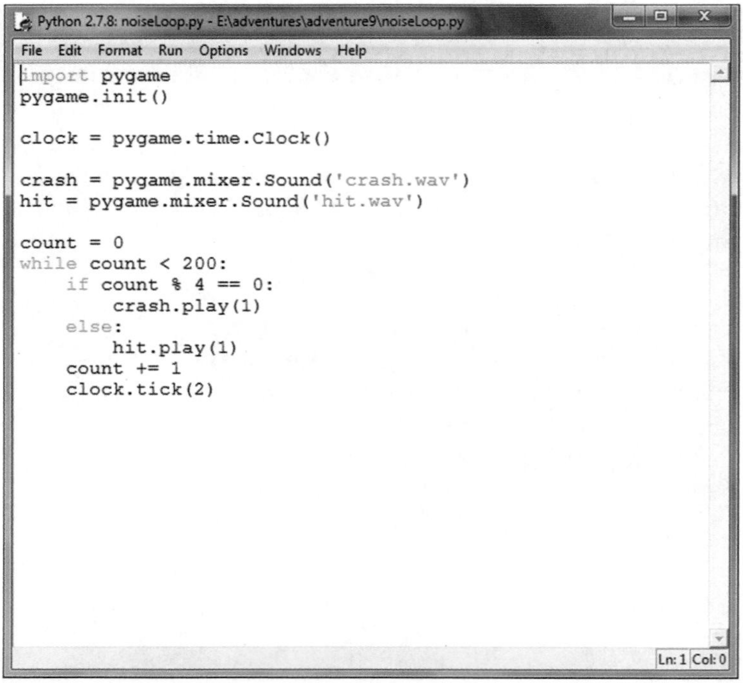

```
Python 2.7.8: noiseLoop.py - E:\adventures\adventure9\noiseLoop.py

File  Edit  Format  Run  Options  Windows  Help

import pygame
pygame.init()

clock = pygame.time.Clock()

crash = pygame.mixer.Sound('crash.wav')
hit = pygame.mixer.Sound('hit.wav')

count = 0
while count < 200:
    if count % 4 == 0:
        crash.play(1)
    else:
        hit.play(1)
    count += 1
    clock.tick(2)

                                                         Ln: 1 Col: 0
```

FIGURE 9-2 Running this program will play a loop of sounds. Every fourth sound will be different from the other three.

4. The next statement creates the clock. Although the program doesn't use a window or animations, it still uses the clock. The clock will determine how fast the sounds play later in the program. Add this to your program:

```
clock = pygame.time.Clock()
```

5. You're going to use two sounds in this program, crash.wav and hit.wav. The program now needs to load these sounds:

```
crash = pygame.mixer.Sound('crash.wav')
hit = pygame.mixer.Sound('hit.wav')
```

6. The next part of the program creates the count and the loop. The loop limits the number of times it repeats so that it only plays 200 sounds before closing:

```
count = 0
while count < 200:
```

7. As the loop repeats, the crash sound will play every fourth repeat in the loop. The next bit of code controls this:

```
    if count % 4 == 0:
        crash.play()
```

Remember back to Adventure 2 when you were introduced to the modulo operator? The modulo % operator is used like the division operator, except that instead of dividing one number by another, it calculates the remainder after one number has been divided by another. For example, 7 divided by 3 divides twice with a remainder of 1. Therefore 7 % 3 would evaluate to 1. To work out if a number is a multiple of another, the modulo operator is used with the equal to == comparator. For example, in the program above, count % 4 == 0 checks if the count is a multiple of 4, so that the program plays the sound every fourth time the loop repeats.

8. The hit sound will play whenever the crash sound doesn't play—in other words, three times every loop:

```
else:
    hit.play()
```

9. The last lines of the code increase the count every time the loop repeats and limit the speed that the loop repeats. In this case, it will repeat twice a second:

```
count += 1
clock.tick(2)
```

10. Save the program and run it using Run⇨Run Module.

11. When the program starts running it plays the sounds in a loop. What does it sound like? Every fourth sound should be a crash, and the other three should be hit sounds.

You might notice that the timing of the sounds isn't great! The delay between each sound has a slight variation. This is because the clock.tick() and play() functions don't keep timings very well.

Making Keyboard Sound Effects

For a video that walks you through the steps of using the keyboard to control sounds, visit the companion website at www.wiley.com/go/adventuresinpython. Click the Videos tab and select the appropriate file.

In this program, you'll use the keyboard to control sounds (see Figure 9-3). When you press the a or s key, it will play a sound. You can add your own sounds and keys by extending the program.

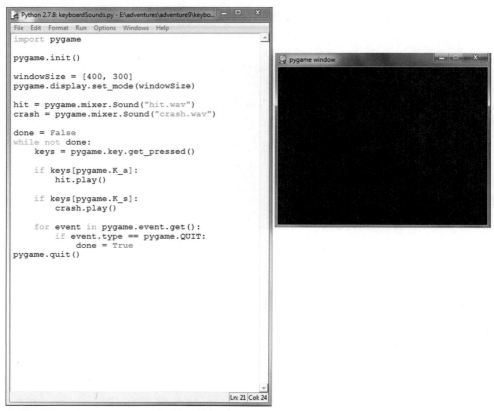

```
import pygame

pygame.init()

windowSize = [400, 300]
pygame.display.set_mode(windowSize)

hit = pygame.mixer.Sound("hit.wav")
crash = pygame.mixer.Sound("crash.wav")

done = False
while not done:
    keys = pygame.key.get_pressed()

    if keys[pygame.K_a]:
        hit.play()

    if keys[pygame.K_s]:
        crash.play()

    for event in pygame.event.get():
        if event.type == pygame.QUIT:
            done = True
pygame.quit()
```

FIGURE 9-3 Pressing the a and s keys will now play sounds.

Adding sounds when keys are pressed is used in many video games. For example, in fantasy adventure games characters make a noise when they swing their sword, fire their bow or cast a spell.

1. Open IDLE and create a new file with File⇨New Window.

2. Save the program as keyboardSounds.py in the Adventure 9 folder.

3. Add the first two lines to the program that allow it to use PyGame in the program:

```
import pygame
pygame.init()
```

4. This program uses a window, as it also uses the keyboard, so set up the window now with this code:

```
windowSize = [400, 300]
pygame.display.set_mode(windowSize)
```

5. Now you're ready to load the sounds:

```
hit = pygame.mixer.Sound("hit.wav")
```

Be careful that the filename is correct, otherwise the program may not work as you expect.

```
crash = pygame.mixer.Sound("crash.wav")
```

6. This code starts the game loop:

```
done = False
while not done:
```

7. The next bit of code checks if keys are pressed and plays the sounds if they are:

```
    keys = pygame.key.get_pressed()

    if keys[pygame.K_a]:
        hit.play()

    if keys[pygame.K_s]:
        crash.play()
```

8. Now add the code to manage the closing of the window:

```
    for event in pygame.event.get():
        if event.type == pygame.QUIT:
            done = True
pygame.quit()
```

9. Save the program and run it using Run⇨Run Module.

10. When the window opens, click on it and press the a and s keys. You should hear the hit and crash sounds. Have some fun with that, but watch out—if you press the keys really quickly, sometimes the sound won't play.

CRAIG SAYS...

You can mix and match parts of Python and PyGame programs. For example, you've just written a program that combines the keyboard and sounds. Later in this adventure, you'll learn how to use sounds with Tkinter and learn how to combine sounds with the sprite program you made in Adventure 8.

Using Music with Python

You're now going to learn how to use music with PyGame and Python. PyGame's music features work slightly differently than its sound features, and some of the functions vary slightly from the sound functions. Also, only one music file can be loaded at a time, unlike sounds, which can have several loaded at once.

Games use music really well to help set the mood and feel of the game. For example, in mystery games, tense and dramatic music is used to build suspense. Fantasy games often use music that features older, folk instruments and avoid modern music. You'll create a program that plays a single music file, a file that adds a wobbling volume effect to the sound and a GUI that can control the volume of the music and pause it.

Playing Music

VIDEO

For a video that walks you through the steps of playing music in your game, visit the companion website at www.wiley.com/go/adventuresinpython. Click the Videos tab and select the appropriate file.

This first program will get you used to using music with PyGame and Python (see Figure 9-4). It will play a single music file. Like the sound programs you created earlier, it won't open a window when the program runs.

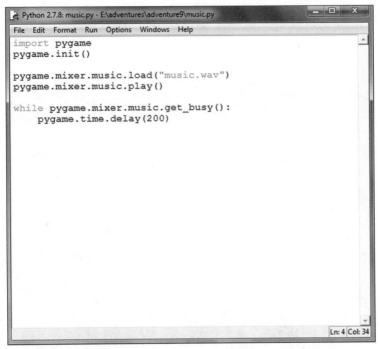

FIGURE 9-4 The code to play music in PyGame

1. Open IDLE and create a new file with File⇨New Window.

2. Save the program as `music.py` in the `Adventure 9` folder.

3. First you need to add the two statements that allow the program to use PyGame:

```
import pygame
pygame.init()
```

4. The next part of the program loads the music and plays it:

```
pygame.mixer.music.load("music.mp3")
pygame.mixer.music.play()
```

5. Just like playing the sounds earlier, the program will close instantly before the music plays unless you add some code to keep it open. This next piece of code uses a loop to make the program stay open while the music is playing:

```
while pygame.mixer.music.get_busy():
    pygame.time.wait(200)
```

6. Save the program and run it using Run⇨Run Module.

7. When the program starts, it will play the music once and then close.

DIGGING INTO THE CODE

In PyGame, using music is slightly different to using sounds. Whereas when sounds are used with PyGame the entire file is loaded at once, when music is used only part of the file is loaded, and the rest of it is loaded as the music progresses. This is so that the program can load larger files without using up too much memory.

In the program you've just created, the load() function is used to load the music. Unlike sounds, only one song can be loaded at any time. The play() function plays the music that is loaded, you won't be surprised to hear!

Like the program that played sounds earlier in this adventure, sometimes the program will close before the music has played in full. In this program, pygame. mixer.music.get_busy() states whether there is music currently playing. This function is used as a condition of the while loop in this program. If a sound is playing, the while loop will repeat, stopping the program from closing. When the music stops playing the loop will stop repeating, and therefore the program will close as well.

Adding Volume Tremolo

For a video that walks you through the steps of adding tremolo to your game, visit the companion website at www.wiley.com/go/adventuresinpython. Click the Videos tab and select the appropriate file.

Next, you're going to add tremolo to some music (see Figure 9-5).

```
Python 2.7.8: tremolo.py - E:\adventures\adventure9\tremolo.py

File  Edit  Format  Run  Options  Windows  Help

import math
import pygame
pygame.init()

pygame.mixer.music.load("music.mp3")
pygame.mixer.music.play()

count = 0
while pygame.mixer.music.get_busy():
    volume = abs(math.sin(count))
    pygame.mixer.music.set_volume(volume)
    count += 0.2
    print volume
    pygame.time.delay(200)
```

FIGURE 9-5 When the music plays, the volume goes up and down in a wave.

Tremolo is a sound effect where the volume of the sound increases and decreases in waves. As the music plays, the volume of the music will increase and decrease, just as if you were turning the volume up and down really quickly.

Tremolo has many uses in music. If the speed of the effect is really fast, it sounds choppy. Effects like this have some use in computer games. Tremolos can be used to make things sound spooky or exciting, depending on the speed.

1. Open IDLE and create a new Python program with File⇨New Window.

2. Save the program as `tremolo.py` in the `Adventure 9` folder.

3. Click in the file editor and add this code to allow your program to use `PyGame` and the `math` module. The `math` module is used later in the program to add the tremolo wobble to the music:

```
import math
import pygame
pygame.init()
```

4. The next part of the program loads and plays the music:

```
pygame.mixer.music.load("music.mp3")
pygame.mixer.music.play()
```

5. This part of the program starts the loop that applies the tremolo wobble to the music. The count isn't used to control the number of times the loop repeats, but instead is used to set the level of the volume in the tremolo:

```
count = 0
while pygame.mixer.music.get_busy():
```

6. Inside the loop, the volume level is determined using the first statement in this code. The `sin()` function creates the wave used to set the volume and the `abs()` function makes sure the value is positive:

```
    volume = abs(math.sin(count))
```

7. Next, the volume is set and there is a delay before the next loop starts:

```
pygame.mixer.music.set_volume(volume)
    count += 0.2
    pygame.time.delay(200)
```

8. Save the program and run it using Run⇨Run Module.

9. When the program starts the music will play, with the volume increasing and decreasing in a wave.

DIGGING INTO THE CODE

The `math.sin()` function you just used returns the sine of a number. You don't need to understand how this works exactly, you just need to know that it returns values in a wave shape. When the values increase they are returned so that they move in a predictable wave. This is what gives the program the volume increases and decreases in a wave. The function can return positive and negative values, so to make sure that the volume is always positive in this program, the `abs()` function is used.

With music, the volume can be set using the `pygame.mixer.music.set_volume()` function. It takes an argument between 0 and 1, with 1 being full volume.

Making a Music Player

Now for something really exciting. In this next program you'll use `Tkinter` and `PyGame` together to make a music player (see Figure 9-6). Your program will create a GUI that allows you to play and pause a song using a button and control its volume with a slider.

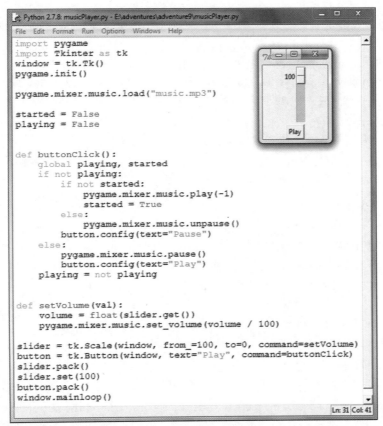

FIGURE 9-6 The code for a superb basic music player, complete with control button and volume slider, which plays a single song on a loop.

1. Start as usual by opening IDLE and creating a new file with File⇨New Window.

2. Save the program as `musicPlayer.py` in the `Adventure 9` folder.

3. The first part of the program allows it to use `PyGame` and `Tkinter`. This code is no different to the code you'd use for `PyGame` or `Tkinter` individually:

```python
import pygame
import Tkinter as tk
window = tk.Tk()
pygame.init()
```

4. Next up, add this statement to the program to load the music file:

```
pygame.mixer.music.load("music.mp3")
```

5. The next two variables are used later in the program to check whether the music has started playing and whether the music is paused. As the music hasn't started at this point in the program, both of the variables are set to False:

```
started = False
playing = False
```

6. So that the button in the program can run code when it is clicked, this program includes these functions to check if the music has started, is playing or has been paused, then plays or pauses the music. The first part of the program makes the playing and started variables global so that the function can change their values:

```
def buttonClick():
    global playing, started
```

7. The next part of the function checks if the music is not playing. This means that the music is either paused or hasn't started playing yet:

```
if not playing:
```

8. In the next bit of code, if the music hasn't started playing yet (in other words, the Play button hasn't been clicked yet), the program will start to play the music:

```
if not started:
    pygame.mixer.music.play(-1)
    started = True
```

9. If the music has started playing but isn't currently playing, the music must therefore be paused. This code will un-pause the music:

```
else:
    pygame.mixer.music.unpause()
```

10. When the music is paused, this piece of code changes the text on the button to Pause:

```
button.config(text="Pause")
```

11. If the music is playing, the next piece of code changes the button's text to Play and pauses the music when the button is next pressed:

```
else:
    pygame.mixer.music.pause()
    button.config(text="Play")
```

12. The next bit of code either stops or starts the music, depending on if it was or wasn't playing already. If it was `True` (it was playing), it will be swapped to `False` (stops playing) and vice versa.

```
playing = not playing
```

13. The next function changes the volume when the slider updates. You're going to create a volume slider in the next step, which returns a number between 0 and 100—but the `volume_set()` function requires a number between 0 and 1. For that reason, the last statement in this function divides the slider's value by 100 so that it is the right size:

```
def setVolume(val):
    volume = float(slider.get())
    pygame.mixer.music.set_volume(volume / 100)
```

14. Next, you need to create the button and the slider for the program. For this, a `Tkinter` button and a `Tkinter` scale object are used. While it's possible to make these things in `PyGame`, they have already been built into `Tkinter` to make it much quicker and easier for you to use them:

```
slider = tk.Scale(window, from_=100, to=0, command=setVolume)
button = tk.Button(window, text="Play", command=buttonClick)
```

15. Finally, this piece of code adds the slider and button to the window and starts the `Tkinter` main loop:

```
slider.pack()
slider.set(100)
button.pack()
window.mainloop()
```

16. Save the program and run it using Run⇨Run Module.

17. It's time to test your handiwork! Click the buttons to play and pause the music and change the volume with the slider.

CRAIG SAYS.

This program demonstrates how you can mix and match functions from different Python modules. You can use all the `PyGame` sound and music functions with `Tkinter`. There are many ways you can mix and match `PyGame` and `Tkinter` but you can't use any of their GUI elements together at the same time. For example, you can't use `PyGame` windows simultaneously in the same windows with `Tkinter` GUIs. Have some fun trying out using `PyGame` sounds and music in different ways with `Tkinter`.

Adding Sounds and Music to a Game

In Adventure 8, you created a very basic game where a sprite walks around the window. With a few slight changes to the program, you can add music and sounds, which will add sophistication and polish to your game.

In this program, you'll modify the sprite walking program to add background music and a sound effect when the sprite teleports.

1. Open the game that you created in Adventure 8. You should have saved it as `walkingSprite.py`.

2. When the file opens, find this statement:

```
white = pygame.color.Color("#FFFFFF")
```

3. Directly below that statement, add the following code to load and play the music and to load the sound when the sprite teleports:

```
pygame.mixer.music.load("music.mp3")
pygame.mixer.music.play(-1)
teleportSound = pygame.mixer.Sound("teleport.wav")
```

4. Next, find these lines of code that teleport the player to a new location:

```
if count < 5:
    image = teleport1
elif count < 10:
    image = teleport2
```

5. Directly above that code, add this to play the teleport sound. You use the `if` statement so that the sound only plays once at the start of the loop:

```
if count == 0:
    teleportSound.play()
else:
    x = random.randrange(0, windowSize[0])
    y = random.randrange(0, windowSize[1])
    count = -1
    locked = False
count += 1
```

6. Save the program and run it using Run➪Run Module.

7. When the program starts, the background music will begin playing on a loop.

8. In the game, press the space bar to teleport the player. Magic! The teleport will make a sound. You can see the completed game in Figure 9-7.

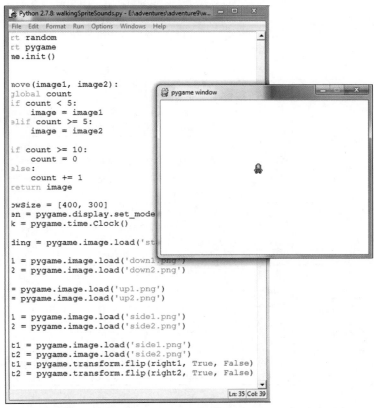

```
rt random
rt pygame
ne.init()


nove(image1, image2):
global count
if count < 5:
    image = image1
alif count >= 5:
    image = image2

if count >= 10:
    count = 0
alse:
    count += 1
return image

owSize = [400, 300]
en = pygame.display.set_mode
k = pygame.time.Clock()

ling = pygame.image.load('st

1 = pygame.image.load('down1.png')
2 = pygame.image.load('down2.png')

= pygame.image.load('up1.png')
= pygame.image.load('up2.png')

1 = pygame.image.load('side1.png')
2 = pygame.image.load('side2.png')

t1 = pygame.image.load('side1.png')
t2 = pygame.image.load('side2.png')
t1 = pygame.transform.flip(right1, True, False)
t2 = pygame.transform.flip(right2, True, False)
```

Ln: 35 Col: 39

FIGURE 9-7 The sprite program now features sounds and music.

CHALLENGE

With only a few changes to your programs you can add sounds and music. In this example, you learned how to add sounds to games. Try going back to some of the programs you made in earlier adventures and adding sounds and music to them too.

Python Command Quick Reference Table

Command	Description
sound = pygame.mixer.Sound(file)	This function is used to load a sound. The filename of the sound is used as an argument. Once the file is loaded, it can be stored in a variable.
sound.play()	To play a sound that has been loaded using the load() function, the play() function is used.
pygame.time.delay()	Instead of you having to import the time module to use with PyGame, PyGame has inbuilt functions that do the same things. This function will make the program wait for a number of milliseconds. The time to wait is given as an argument. There are 1000 milliseconds in 1 second.
sound.get_length()	This function returns the length of a sound in seconds. By dividing it by 1000, you can convert it to milliseconds.
Modulo %	The modulo operator divides one number by another and returns the remainder from the division.
pygame.mixer.music.load()	In PyGame, the load() function is used to load music into the program. The filename is used as an argument to state which sound file will be loaded. Only one music file can be loaded at a time.
pygame.mixer.music.play()	This function is used to play a loaded music file. If you use -1 as an argument, the music will repeat forever.
pygame.mixer.music.get_busy()	When music is playing, this function will return True, and when no music is playing, it will return False.
abs()	The abs() function makes a negative number positive.
pygame.mixer.music.set_volume()	This function is used to set the volume of the PyGame music. The argument should be between 0.0 and 1.0.

Achievement Unlocked: Skilled manipulator of sound and music in Python and PyGame programs.

Next Adventure

Hooray! You've learned how to use sounds and music with `PyGame` and Python. You've created some cool programs and have learned some tools to help you create programs that use sound.

In the next and final adventure, you'll make a game by incorporating many of the tips and tricks you've learned throughout the adventures in this book!

Adventure **10**
Your Really Big Adventure

CONGRATULATIONS—YOU'VE REACHED your final adventure! You've come a very long way and learned a lot about Python. You've learned about Python programming concepts including variables, `if` statements, functions, `while` loops, `for` loops, lists and comparators. You've also been introduced to different Python libraries including the `turtle` module, `Tkinter` and `PyGame`.

In this final adventure, you will combine lots of the things you learned about Python in your previous adventures to create a fantastic two-player game. So, what does this program do? It's a game in which two players compete to collect coins. The coins' locations are randomly generated and change every time a coin is collected. The players' scores are displayed next to the player sprites.

Players can move in eight directions (up, down, left, right and diagonally in four ways). If players collide, they bounce in opposite directions. There are walls around the edge of the game that stop the players walking off the edge of the window. There are four doors in the walls, through which players can move. Leaving through one door makes them reappear in the opposite door.

You control the players using a single keyboard. The w, a, s and d keys control player 1, and the up, down, left and right keys control player 2.

You can see the finished game in Figure 10-1.

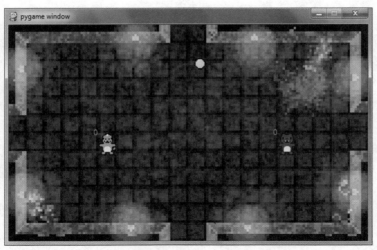

FIGURE 10-1 In the finished game, two players compete to collect coins.

Writing the Program for the Game

This is the most complex of all the programs in this book, and it's a long one—almost 300 lines long! Don't be put off, though. It's easier than you think because you've seen everything in the program before, in your earlier adventures. The program combines things that you've seen with Python and PyGame, including music, sounds, images and the keyboard.

You've covered all of the Python code used here in previous adventures. As you move through the coding, I'll tell you where you first encountered the Python code so that you can look back at previous adventures if you need to in order to remind yourself how things work.

Setting Up the Files

This adventure requires several files for sprites and sounds. You'll find instructions on how to set up the files in the Appendix.

You can also design your own sprites and background for the game. Use the default images for the program as a template for designing your own. If you keep the same size of sprites and the same size of background, this program will work exactly the same. If you change the size of anything, however, you will need to modify other things in the program, such as the functions that check whether a player is walking into a wall or touching a coin.

Make sure the images and sounds are in the correct folder. You should have the following files:

- background.png

- coin.png

- coin.wav

- light.png

- music.mp3

- sprite1_standing.png

- sprite1_walking1.png

- sprite1_walking2.png

- sprite2_standing.png

- sprite2_walking1.png

- sprite2_walking2.png

If you don't have these files, follow the steps in the appendix to add them before continuing.

Making the Game

Now you can start making the game by following the steps in this section. As the game has two players, it makes sense to make the code reusable using functions. This will make the program more manageable and, as the same functions can be used for each player, it means you won't have to duplicate the code for each player. The first part of the program defines the functions. Follow the instructions to start creating the game:

1. Open IDLE and create a new file with File⇨New Window.

2. Save the program as bigGame.py in the Adventure 10 folder.

3. In the file editor, add this code to import the PyGame module and the random module:

```
import random
import pygame
pygame.init()
```

4. The next part of the program adds a function that is used to determine which image will be used in the sprite's walking animation. Add this to your program now:

```
def moveAnimation(image1, image2, count):
    if 10 < count % 20 <= 20:
        return image2
    else:
        return image1
```

 CRAIG SAYS... You need three sprites for each player in this game: one for when the player is standing still and two for the movement animation. Unlike the program in Adventure 8, which had sprites for every direction in which the player could walk, this program only has sprites for one direction. This means the player faces the same direction all the time, no matter which direction they are heading. You can see the sprites used for this game in Figure 10-2.

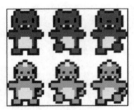

FIGURE 10-2 All the player sprites used in the game

Walls

There are walls in the game which the player shouldn't be able to walk through. To handle this, you need to include functions to stop the player moving through the walls. The walls are shown on the background, which you can see in Figure 10-3. This code stops the players from walking over the area of the background where the walls are located. Follow these steps:

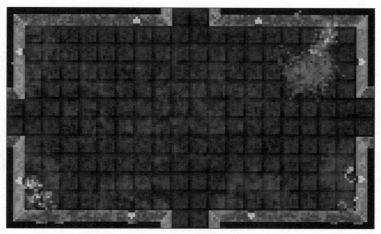

FIGURE 10-3 The game's background

1. Select the line below the last function in your program.

2. This first function checks whether the player can move upwards or there is a wall in the way. The function returns 1 if the player can move and 0 if they can't. These numbers are used later in the program and determine the distance the player moves. The single function will stop the player moving through the top wall as well as through the wall above two of the four doors. Add it to your program now:

```
def upClear(x, y):
    canMove = True

    if verticalDoorLeft <= x <= verticalDoorRight and ↵
      y - 1 < topWall:
        canMove = True
    elif y - 1 < topWall:
        canMove = False
    elif (x < leftWall or x > rightWall) and y - 1 < ↵
      middleDoorsTop:
        canMove = False

    if canMove:
        return 1
    else:
        return 0
```

3. Like the upClear() function, the downClear() function checks whether the player can move downwards or whether there is a wall in the way:

```python
def downClear(x, y):
    canMove = True

    if verticalDoorLeft <= x <= verticalDoorRight and ↵
      bottomWall < y + 1:
        canMove = True
    elif bottomWall < y + 1:
        canMove = False
    elif (x < leftWall or x > rightWall) and y + 1 > ↵
      middleDoorsBottom:
        canMove = False

    if canMove:
        return 1
    else:
        return 0
```

4. The leftClear() function checks whether the player can move left or whether there is a wall in the way:

```python
def leftClear(x, y):
    canMove = True

    if middleDoorsTop <= y <= middleDoorsBottom and ↵
      x - 1 < leftWall:
        canMove = True
    elif x - 1 < leftWall:
        canMove = False
    elif (y > bottomWall or y < topWall) and x - 1 < ↵
      verticalDoorLeft:
        canMove = False

    if canMove:
        return 1
    else:
        return 0
```

5. Finally, the rightClear() function checks whether the player can move to the right or whether there is a wall in the way:

```python
def rightClear(x, y):
    canMove = True

    if middleDoorsTop <= y <= middleDoorsBottom and ↵
      x + 1 > rightWall:
        canMove = True
```

```
        elif x + 1 > rightWall:
            canMove = False
        elif (y > bottomWall or y < topWall) and x + 1 > ↵
          verticalDoorRight:
            canMove = False

        if canMove:
            return 1
        else:
            return 0
```

Doors, Collisions and Coins

The next functions in your program are used to check when the player walks through a door, whether the players have collided and whether the player is touching a coin.

1. Add a new line below the code you've already added to the program.

2. The first function will check if the player has moved through one of the doors. If the player has moved through a door, it will return new x and y coordinates for the player, which will move the player to the opposite door in the game.

```
def checkOffscreen(x, y):
    if x < -14:
        x = windowSize[0] - 14
    elif x > windowSize[0] - 14:
        x = -14

    if y < -20:
        y = windowSize[1] - 20
    elif y > windowSize[1] - 20:
        y = -20
    return x, y
```

DIGGING INTO THE CODE

The code for this part of the program uses functions and range checks. You met functions for the first time in Adventure 2, when you created your own functions with the turtle module. Range checks were introduced in Adventure 6.

The background has walls and doors. The range checks in this part of the program determine whether the player is walking into a wall or a door. You can see the background in Figure 10-3. The "blue smudge" in the top-right corner of the background is water. It's probably not the best water you've ever seen, but it doesn't affect how the game is played in any way.

3. The next part of the program checks whether the players are touching. If they are, they should push each other away in opposite directions. So that the players aren't pushed through walls, the distance the players move is set using two loops, one for the x coordinates and the other for the y coordinates. Each loop checks whether the player can continue to move in that direction, adding 1 to the distance they travel if they can and 0 if they can't. Add this code to your program now:

```python
def playersTouching():
    global pOneX, pOneY, pTwoX, pTwoY

    if -32 < pOneX - pTwoX < 32 and -40 < pOneY - pTwoY < 40:
        xDiff = pOneX - pTwoX
        yDiff = pOneY - pTwoY

        for dist in range(abs(xDiff) / 2):
            pOneMove = leftClear(pOneX, pOneY) + ↵
              rightClear(pOneX, pOneY)
            pTwoMove = leftClear(pTwoX, pTwoY) + ↵
              rightClear(pTwoX, pTwoY)
            if xDiff > 0:
                pOneX += pOneMove / 2 * xDiff / xDiff
                pTwoX -= pTwoMove / 2 * xDiff / xDiff
            else:
                pOneX -= pOneMove / 2 * xDiff / xDiff
                pTwoX += pTwoMove / 2 * xDiff / xDiff

        for dist in range(abs(yDiff) / 2):
            pOneMove = upClear(pOneX, pOneY) + ↵
              downClear(pOneX, pOneY)
            pTwoMove = upClear(pTwoX, pTwoY) + ↵
              downClear(pTwoX, pTwoY)
            if yDiff > 0:
                pOneY += pOneMove / 2 * yDiff / yDiff
                pTwoY -= pTwoMove / 2 * yDiff / yDiff
            else:
                pOneY -= pOneMove / 2 * yDiff / yDiff
                pTwoY += pTwoMove / 2 * yDiff / yDiff
```

4. The next function checks whether a player is touching the coin by checking if their position is near the coin. The function will return True if they are and False if they aren't. This function does not add points to the players' scores or reset the coin's position; this is done later in the program. Add this function to your program now:

```python
def touchingCoin(x, y):
    return -32 < x - coinPos[0] < 20 and -40 < ↵
      y - coinPos[1] < 20
```

The parts of the program that decide how far the player should move use `for` loops. `For` loops were introduced in Adventure 2, so have a look at that adventure if you need to revise `for` loops.

The position of the player is set at the top-left corner of the sprite. This can cause some problems when walking through doors using the `checkOffScreen()` function. If the window's size was used for the left door, the player would need to move the entire sprite off the right side of the screen for the door to detect it. On the other side of the screen if the value 0 was used, the player would need to only touch the door slightly for it to be detected. When developing the game this looked a bit odd, therefore the number -14 (instead of 0) was used to check if the player touched the left door and the window's size minus 14 was used for the right door. 14 is half of the player's width (28 pixels) so this makes moving through doors look a bit more normal as half of the player must move through the door before they are moved. This is the same for the top and bottom doors, but the value -20 is used as 20 is half of the player's height.

For the `randomPosition()` function, the coin should not be placed in the walls, otherwise the players will not be able to collect it. To avoid this the lowest argument of the `randrange()` function is the width of the wall and the highest value argument is the width of the wall plus the width of the coin. This stops the coin getting stuck in the walls, but it will also not appear in any doors.

5. The last function generates a random position for the coin. This is used to set its original position and a new position when the coin is collected. In the file editor, add this code to your program:

```
def randomPosition():
    x = random.randrange(32, windowSize[0] - 52)
    y = random.randrange(32, windowSize[1] - 52)
    return x, y
```

Setting Up the Window and Variables

Now that the program has all the functions needed in the game, it's time to add variables and other Python code to join it all together.

The next part of the program sets up the size of the window, followed by variables for displaying text, player positions, images and sounds:

1. Select the line below the code you added in the section above.

2. Add this code to set up the window size and the clock for the game:

```
windowSize = [640, 384]
screen = pygame.display.set_mode(windowSize)
clock = pygame.time.Clock()
```

DEFINITIONS

A **font** sets the look of text. A font contains every letter and number and how they should be displayed in your program or document. There are thousands of fonts in the world, and they change the look of text.

A **monospaced** font is a category of font where every letter, number and symbol is exactly the same width. Monospaced fonts are most often used to format code. They are also useful for displaying points and other information as you can predict the width of the text and get a consistent size.

3. The next part of the program sets the font in which the points will be displayed. Each character in a monospace font is the same size, which makes it much easier to know how much space the points will take up when they are displayed above the players' heads. Add this code to your program now:

```
# Font for points
pointFont = pygame.font.SysFont("Monospace", 15)
```

4. The next set of variables sets the players' starting positions, the coin's starting position, the points collected by each player and variables that are used when animating the players. Add this code now:

```
# Variables for position etc.
pOneX = windowSize[0] / 4
pOneY = windowSize[1] / 2

pTwoX = (windowSize[0] / 4) * 3
pTwoY = windowSize[1] / 2

coinPos = randomPosition()

pOnePoints = 0
pTwoPoints = 0

pOneCount = 0
pTwoCount = 0

pOneMoving = False
pTwoMoving = False
```

5. The next part of the program sets the values for the wall and door locations. These variables are used in the functions that check whether the players have walked into walls or are going through doors. Add these variables to your program now:

```
# Variables for walls
leftWall = 28
topWall = 16
rightWall = windowSize[0] - 60
bottomWall = 312

middleDoorsTop = 144
middleDoorsBottom = 182
verticalDoorLeft = 284
verticalDoorRight = verticalDoorLeft + 40
```

6. The next set of variables store the loaded images for the background, all the player animation sprites and the coin. All the images are resized to make them look retro and pixelated. The image stored in the light variable is used for lights in the game. Later in the program, it is placed over all the other images so that it looks like a light is shining on them. Add the code to load the images now:

```
# Load images
background = pygame.image.load("background.png")
background = pygame.transform.scale(background, windowSize)

light = pygame.image.load("light.png")
light = pygame.transform.scale(light, windowSize)

pOneMove1 = pygame.image.load("sprite1_walking1.png")
pOneMove1 = pygame.transform.scale2x(pOneMove1)

pOneMove2 = pygame.image.load("sprite1_walking2.png")
pOneMove2 = pygame.transform.scale2x(pOneMove2)

pOneStanding = pygame.image.load("sprite1_standing.png")
pOneStanding = pygame.transform.scale2x(pOneStanding)

pTwoMove1 = pygame.image.load("sprite2_walking1.png")
pTwoMove1 = pygame.transform.scale2x(pTwoMove1)

pTwoMove2 = pygame.image.load("sprite2_walking2.png")
pTwoMove2 = pygame.transform.scale2x(pTwoMove2)

pTwoStanding = pygame.image.load("sprite2_standing.png")
pTwoStanding = pygame.transform.scale2x(pTwoStanding)

coin = pygame.image.load("coin.png")
coin = pygame.transform.scale2x(coin)
```

7. The final set of variables loads the coin collect sound and game music into the program. Add it now:

```
# Load music and sound
coinSound = pygame.mixer.Sound("coin.wav")
pygame.mixer.music.load("music.mp3")
pygame.mixer.music.play(-1)
```

You used images with PyGame in Adventure 8. The rest of the code that uses images and blits them to the window comes later in this the adventure. In addition to the background image, a layer for light is also loaded. This layer is semi-transparent so that it looks like the light is shining on the sprites. Semi-transparent means that some of the pixels are not entirely solid and you can see through them like coloured glass.

Adding the Game Loop

The remaining part of the program runs the game loop. The main purpose of this loop is to respond to the keys pressed by both players, animate the player sprites, check whether the players are touching, check whether a player has collected coins, display the points and blit the images to the window. To do all this, the game loop uses all the functions created earlier in the program.

Once you have added the whole game loop to the program you can run the game!

Character Controls and Animations

The first part of the game loop enables the program to check whether any keys have been pressed. It also calls the functions that check whether the player is walking into a wall and determine what sprite is to be used in the animation.

Let's get started.

1. Select the line below the code you added in the last section.

2. The game loop starts in the usual way. Add this code to your program now:

```
# Game loop
done = False
while not done:
```

3. At the start of the game loop, the program checks whether any keys have been pressed. If the w, a, s or d keys have been pressed, the program will move player 1. Add this code to your program now:

```
# Get movement
# Player 1 movement
pOneMoving = False
keys = pygame.key.get_pressed()
if keys[pygame.K_s]:
    pOneY += downClear(pOneX, pOneY)
    pOneMoving = True
if keys[pygame.K_w]:
    pOneY -= upClear(pOneX, pOneY)
    pOneMoving = True
if keys[pygame.K_a]:
    pOneX -= leftClear(pOneX, pOneY)
    pOneMoving = True
if keys[pygame.K_d]:
    pOneX += rightClear(pOneX, pOneY)
    pOneMoving = True


pOneX, pOneY = checkOffscreen(pOneX, pOneY)
```

4. To decide which image is displayed for player 1, the program checks whether the player is moving. If it is moving, the program uses the moveAnimation() function to determine which sprite should be displayed for the animation. If the player isn't moving, it displays the standing sprite. Add the code now:

```
# Player 1 animation
if pOneMoving:
    pOneCount += 1
    pOneImage = moveAnimation(pOneMove1, pOneMove2, ↩
      pOneCount)
else:
    pOneImage = pOneStanding
```

5. The code for player 2 is very similar to the code for player 1 but just uses different keys for movement and different images for the animation. Add this code now:

```
# Player 2 movement
pTwoMoving = False
if keys[pygame.K_DOWN]:
    pTwoY += downClear(pTwoX, pTwoY)
    pTwoMoving = True
if keys[pygame.K_UP]:
    pTwoY -= upClear(pTwoX, pTwoY)
    pTwoMoving = True
if keys[pygame.K_LEFT]:
    pTwoX -= leftClear(pTwoX, pTwoY)
    pTwoMoving = True
```

```
    if keys[pygame.K_RIGHT]:
        pTwoX += rightClear(pTwoX, pTwoY)
        pTwoMoving = True

    pTwoX, pTwoY = checkOffscreen(pTwoX, pTwoY)
```

6. Finally, add the code that animates player 2:

```
# Player 2 animation
if pTwoMoving:
    pTwoCount += 1
    pTwoImage = moveAnimation(pTwoMove1, pTwoMove2, ↵
        pTwoCount)
else:
    pTwoImage = pTwoStanding
```

You were introduced to using the keyboard with PyGame in Adventure 6. There is also similar code to this program in Adventure 8 where you used the keyboard to move a sprite around the window.

You can see the coin in the game in Figure 10-4. As the players move around the game they collect the coins, which adds to their score. In the next section, you will add code to do this.

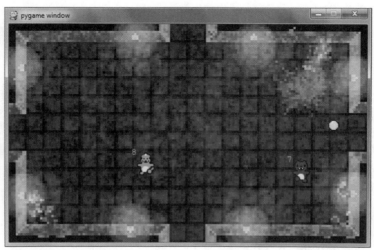

FIGURE 10-4 The players collect coins and gain a point for every coin they collect.

Player Collisions and Collecting Coins

After the player moves, your program needs to check two things: whether the players are touching each other and whether either of them have collected a coin. The `playersTouching()` function is used to check whether the players are touching. The `touchingCoin()` function is used for both players, alongside `if` statements for each player and a final `if` statement that sets the coin's position to a new random location.

1. On the line below the code you've already added to the program, add this code to check whether the players are touching:

   ```
   # Check touching
   playersTouching()
   ```

2. The next part of the program checks whether player 1 is touching the coin and adds a point to their total if they are:

   ```
   # Check touching coin
   if touchingCoin(pOneX, pOneY):
       pOnePoints += 1
       coinSound.play()
   ```

3. After checking whether player 1 is touching the coin, the next few lines of code check whether the other player is touching the coin:

   ```
   if touchingCoin(pTwoX, pTwoY):
       pTwoPoints += 1
       coinSound.play()
   ```

4. If either player is touching the coin, it needs to move to a new random location. Add this code to do that now:

   ```
   # Move coin if touching
   if touchingCoin(pOneX, pOneY) or touchingCoin(pTwoX, ↵
     pTwoY):
   coinPos = randomPosition()
   ```

Displaying Points and Updating the Window

Now that all of the game logic has run in the program, all that's left is to display the points, sprites and background on the window.

1. Click in the window below the rest of your program and create a new line.

2. On the new line, add these lines of code to render the players' points as strings that can be displayed on the PyGame surface:

   ```
   # Render points for display
       pOnePointLabel = pointFont.render(str(pOnePoints), 1,
           (255, 255, 255))
       pTwoPointLabel = pointFont.render(str(pTwoPoints), 1,
           (255, 255, 255))
   ```

3. The next part of the code blits the background, coin, sprites, points and lighting onto the PyGame surface:

```
# Update display
screen.blit(background, (0, 0))
screen.blit(coin, coinPos)
screen.blit(pOneImage, [pOneX, pOneY])
screen.blit(pTwoImage, [pTwoX, pTwoY])
screen.blit(pOnePointLabel, [pOneX - 9, pOneY - 9])
screen.blit(pTwoPointLabel, [pTwoX - 9, pTwoY - 9])
screen.blit(light, (0, 0))

pygame.display.flip()
```

4. The final bit of code allows the window to be closed:

```
# exit
for event in pygame.event.get():
    if event.type == pygame.QUIT:
        done = True
    clock.tick(60)
pygame.quit()
```

Playing the Game

Fantastic! You've finished that long program. It should look something like Figure 10-5.

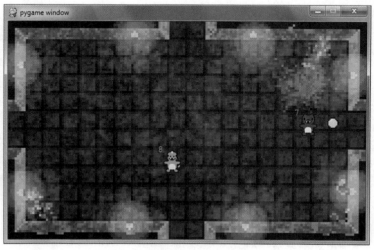

FIGURE 10-5 The finished game

All that remains is for you to play the game. Follow these steps to do so:

1. Click on Run➪Run Module.

2. When the program opens, you can play the game.

3. To move the first player, use the w, a, s and d keys.

4. To move the second player, use the up, down, left and right keys.

5. You'll see the points for each player displayed above the heads of the characters.

Have fun! Test to see if everything works. Can you walk through the wall? Do the doors work? Do you gain points when you walk over the coins?

For a video that shows you the final game in action, visit the companion website at www.wiley.com/go/adventuresinpython. Click the Videos tab and select the appropriate file.

Debugging the Game

No matter how carefully you copied the code, sometimes things just don't work right. This is where your debugging skills come in handy.

There are many different things that can go wrong and a few different strategies you can take to debug things. The first question to ask is whether the bug is stopping the game from running, or if the game is running and the bug is making the game run weirdly?

If the game does not start, you probably get an error message. This is very useful as it will help you identify where the error is coming from. Find the bit of the error message that says something like `"...error on line 35"`. This line is the best place to start looking for the error. Read what type of error you have as well. Did you forget to create a variable? Have you misspelled the name of a function? Did you forget to add a closing bracket or indent some code? Take your time with this and be patient. Even the best of us make mistakes and have to debug our code.

If your game runs and you don't get any error messages, you might be seeing some weird behaviour in the game. For example, one player might be able to walk through walls or you notice that the points aren't added to the total score when coins are collected. This type of bug can be harder to trace. The first question you need to ask yourself is when does the error happen? Does the error happen when the player moves up, when a coin is collected, when the players collide, and so on? If you can identify when

There are many different ways that you can extend the game. Try some of these challenges to test your skills with Python.

Add enemies or obstacles to the game. Make the enemies appear around the game in random positions. When either player collides with the enemy deduct a point. You can also try to add more than one coin to the game.

At the moment the sprites only have two images for their movement animations. Add extra images and animations for the different directions that each player can move. You have already done something similar in Adventure 8.

the error happens, then the piece of code you need to look at is either the function that handles this part of the game or the bit of code in the game loop that handles this part of the game. It also might be the variables that the other parts of the program use. Find these parts and check that your code matches the code in this adventure. Take your time and be patient.

Achievement Unlocked: **Amazing adventurer and creator of a cool computer game.**

Summary

Congratulations! You've reached the end of your adventures in this book. During your journey, you've had a lot of adventures and learned a lot about Python along the way.

You've created programs that use a wide range of fundamental programming concepts with Python. You've learned about variables, functions, `if` statements, `while` loops, `for` loops and lists—among loads of other things. Along the way, you've also become familiar with the Python's `turtle` module, `Tkinter` and `PyGame`.

Well done. You should be very proud of yourself for what you've achieved during your adventures in Python.

I hope you've enjoyed your adventures and have learned a lot along the way. Python programming is a fun and rewarding pursuit, and I wish you all the best in your future adventures! If you're ready for your next big adventure, don't forget about these great resources:

- Full Stack Python (www.fullstackpython.com) is an excellent place for beginners to hone their skills and knowledge. This website has an excellent list of other tutorials you can try with Python, along with other useful programming information.

- Python Weekly (www.pythonweekly.com) is a weekly newsletter that showcases Python tutorials, projects and news. Although some of it may be a bit complex for beginners, you can find lots of interesting tutorials, such as creating your own games and animations.

- Effbot (www.effbot.org/tkinterbook/) has excellent documentation for the `Tkinter` library, which is used in some of the adventures in this book. You might find this website really useful for creating your own programs.

- The book *Adventures in Raspberry Pi*, by Carrie Anne Philbin (ISBN: 978-1-118-75125-1), might be your next step if you want to learn all about the Raspberry Pi.

A

Installing and Downloading the Proper Files

Installing PyGame

For the later adventures in the book you will need to install `PyGame` in order to run the programs. Instructions for installing `PyGame` are given here; just find the section for the operating system you are using and follow the steps.

Windows 8

If you are using Windows 8, follow these steps to install `PyGame`:

1. Open a web browser (such as Internet Explorer, Chrome or Firefox).

2. In the address bar, type `pygame.org/download.shtml` and press the Enter key.

3. When the page loads, scroll down to the Windows section.

4. Click on the `pygame-1.9.1.win32-py2.7.msi` link to begin downloading the file (see Figure A-1).

5. Wait for the download to complete and then open the file.

6. When the installer is open, leave the default choice to Install for all users and click Next.

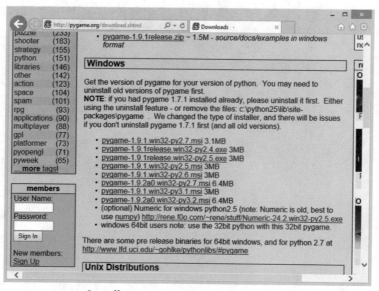

FIGURE A-1 Installing `PyGame` on Windows 8

7. Click Next again.

8. If you are asked if you want to allow the program to make changes to your computer, click Yes.

9. Wait for the installer to complete then click Finish. `PyGame` is now ready to be used (see Figure A-2).

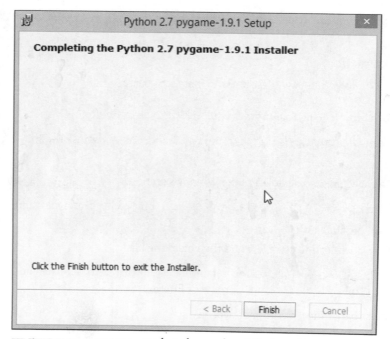

FIGURE A-2 `PyGame` ready to be used on Windows 8

Windows 7

To install PyGame on Windows 7, follow these steps:

1. Open a web browser (such as Internet Explorer, Firefox or Chrome).

2. In the address bar, type `pygame.org/download.shtml` and press the Enter key.

3. When the page has loaded, scroll down to the Windows section and click on the `pygame-1.9.1.win32-py2.7.msi` link to download PyGame (see Figure A-3).

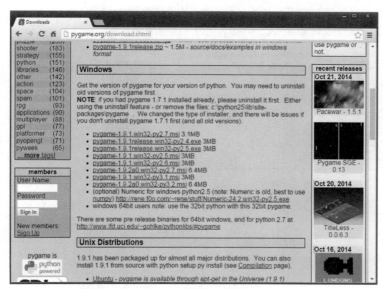

FIGURE A-3 Installing PyGame on Windows 7

4. Once the file has downloaded, open it.

5. When the installer opens, leave the default choice to Install for all users and click Next.

6. Click Next again.

7. If asked if you want to allow the program to make changes to your computer, click Yes.

8. Wait for the installation to complete and then click Finish. PyGame is now ready to be used.

Mac

To install PyGame on your Mac, follow these steps:

1. Open a web browser (such as Safari, Chrome or Firefox).

2. In the address bar of the web browser, type in `pygame.org/download.shtml` and press Enter.

3. Once the webpage has loaded, scroll down to Macintosh.

4. Double-click the first file, which is called `pygame-1.9.1release-python.org-32bit-py2.7-macosx10.3.dmg` (see Figure A-4).

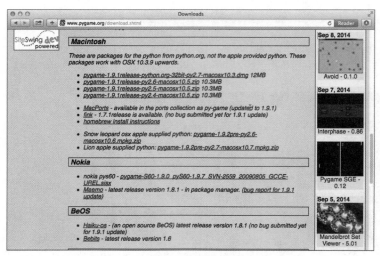

FIGURE A-4 Python packages for Mac

5. Wait for the file to download.

6. Once the file has downloaded, open the `Downloads` folder.

7. Double-click on the file you just downloaded.

8. Right-click on the `mpkg` file and click Open With⇨Installer (see Figure A-5).

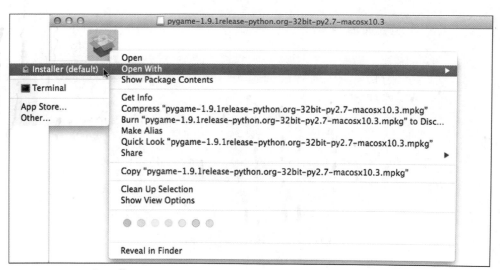

FIGURE A-5 Installing `PyGame` on Mac

9. When the dialog box appears, click Open.

10. Now that the PyGame installer is open, click Continue.

11. Click Continue again.

12. Click Install.

13. If you're asked for your password to give PyGame permission to install, enter your password.

14. Wait for PyGame to install.

15. PyGame has now successfully installed (see Figure A-6).

FIGURE A-6 PyGame ready to be used on Mac

16. Go to the desktop and eject the PyGame disk image by right-clicking the disk image and selecting eject.

Linux (Ubuntu)

To install PyGame on Ubuntu Linux, follow these steps:

1. Open the dashboard and search for the terminal.

2. When the terminal has been found, click on it to open the terminal.

3. Once the terminal has loaded, type in the following command:

```
sudo apt-get update && sudo apt-get upgrade
```

4. If you are asked, type in your password.

5. Press Y if you are asked if you want to install updates.

6. Wait for the update to finish installing.

7. Enter this command to install PyGame (see Figure A-7):

```
sudo apt-get install python-pygame
```

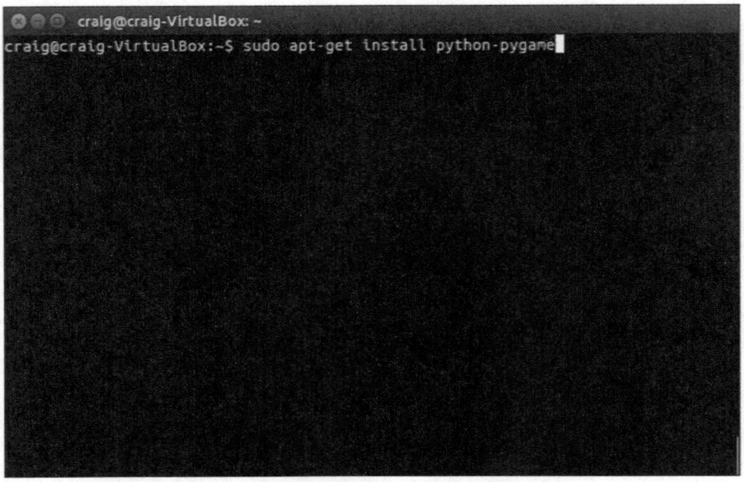

FIGURE A-7 Installing PyGame on Linux

8. Once again, press Y if you are asked if you want to install the new software.

9. Wait until the software finishes installation.

10. When the installation is finished, you can use PyGame with your Python programs.

Raspberry Pi

If you are using Raspbian on your Raspberry Pi, you are in luck—PyGame is already installed by default. This means you don't need to do anything else to use PyGame with Python.

Downloading the Files for Adventures 8, 9 and 10

For Adventures 8, 9 and 10, you are provided with pre-made image and sound files. So that you can use these files with your programs, you need to download them and store them in the same folders/directories as your Python programs. To download the files on your computer, go to the section for your operating system and follow the instructions.

Windows 8

To download the files for your adventures on Windows 8, follow these steps:

1. Open a web browser (such as Internet Explorer, Firefox or Chrome).

2. In the address bar, type www.wiley.com/go/adventuresinpython and press Enter.

3. Scroll down to the link named Downloads and click on it to download the files.

4. Open the folder that the file downloaded to.

5. Right-click on the file and click Extract All...

6. Click Browse and find the `Adventures in Python` folder that you created in the first adventure.

7. Click Extract.

8. The folders and files are now in the correct location for Adventures 8, 9 and 10.

Windows 7

To download the files for your Adventures on Windows 7, follow these steps:

1. Open a web browser (such as Internet Explorer, Firefox or Chrome).

2. In the address bar type www.wiley.com/go/adventuresinpython and press Enter.

3. Scroll down to the link named Downloads and click on it to download the files.

4. Open the folder that the file downloaded to.

5. Right-click on the file and click Extract All...

6. Click Browse and find the `Adventures in Python` folder that you created in the first adventure.

7. Click Extract.

8. The folders and files are now in the correct location for Adventures 8, 9 and 10.

Mac

To download the files for your Adventures on Mac OS X, follow these steps:

1. Open a web browser (such as Safari, Firefox or Chrome).

2. In the address bar, type www.wiley.com/go/adventuresinpython and press Enter.

3. Scroll down to the link named Downloads and click on it to download the files.

4. Open the folder that the file downloaded to.

5. Right-click on the file, move the mouse over Open With and click Archive Utility.

6. Drag the `Adventure 8`, `Adventure 9` and `Adventure 10` folders to the `Adventures in Python` folder that you created in the first adventure.

7. The folders and files are now in the correct location for Adventures 8, 9 and 10.

Linux (Ubuntu)

To download the files for your Adventures on Linux, follow these steps:

1. Open a web browser (such as Firefox or Chromium).
2. In the address bar, type www.wiley.com/go/adventuresinpython and press Enter.
3. Scroll down to the link named Downloads and click on it to download the file.
4. Open the folder that the file downloaded to.
5. Right-click on the file and click Open With Archive Manager.
6. Click Extract and find the `Adventures in Python` folder that you created in the first adventure.
7. Click Extract.
8. The folders and files are now in the correct location for Adventures 8, 9 and 10.

Raspberry Pi

To download the files for your Adventures on Raspberry Pi, follow these steps:

1. Open a web browser (such as Midori or Chromium).
2. In the address bar, type www.wiley.com/go/adventuresinpython and press Enter.
3. Scroll down to the link named Downloads and click on it to download the files.
4. Open the folder that the file downloaded to.
5. Right-click on the file and click Open With Archive Manager.
6. Click Extract and find the `Adventures in Python` folder that you created in the first adventure.
7. Click Extract.
8. The folders and files are now in the correct location for Adventures 8, 9 and 10.

Glossary

anti-aliased line A line that has extra pixels added to make it look smoother. Lines without anti-aliasing are made up of solid pixels and they can look jagged and unsmooth. To make lines look smoother, anti-aliasing adds extra semi-transparent pixels to the lines at certain points and to the line corners.

argument A value that is passed to a function. The value of the argument can change how the function runs.

blit The process of combining two images together by placing one on top of another. The pixels of one image are placed on top of another to create a new image. This is like layering images on top of one another and is used to place images on top of backgrounds.

booleans A data type in Python that have values of either `True` or `False`.

command prompt A visible prompt that indicates that the computer is ready to receive commands from the user. The Python command prompt looks like this: >>> It allows you to input a Python command to be performed.

command-line interfaces (CLI) User interfaces that allow interaction only through text-based commands. They do not respond to mouse input.

comparator Used to compare two values. The *equal to* comparator compares two values to see if they are the same. The comparison will evaluate to either `True` or `False`, depending on whether or not the condition of the comparison is met.

concatenation When a program combines two or more strings together to make a new string.

coordinates Numbers that measure your position. They are used so that a number can be given to location. Coordinates are represented by two numbers, your x coordinate and y coordinate.

cross-platform A cross-platform programming language works on computers with different operating systems. This means you can write a program on one computer, and it will work on most other computers.

data type Determines the values that can be used for variables and other things such as function arguments. For example, the string data type only allows you to use values that are in speech marks, and the integer data type only allows you to use whole numbers.

elif statement Works alongside `if` statements. `elif` is an abbreviation of "else if". Like `if` statements, `elif` statements have their own condition and their code will only run if their condition is `True`. An `elif` statement will also only run if all of the conditions of the `if` and `elif` statements above it are `False`.

else statement Works alongside an `if` statement. The body of an `if` statement will run only if its condition is `True`. On the other hand, the body of the matching `else` statement will only run if the condition of the `if` statement is `False`.

file editor Allows you to create, save and modify programs that contain several lines of Python statements. Unlike a Python shell, there is no command prompt so each statement will not automatically run when you press Enter. Instead, the program will run lines of code in sequence—but not until you tell it to.

float A data type that stores numbers with decimal places. For example, 3.57, 668.1 and 45.5 are all examples of float values.

font Sets the look of text. A font contains every letter and number and how they should be displayed in your program or document. There are thousands of fonts in the world, and they change the look of text.

for loop Used to repeat a block of code a number of times. It will repeat for every item in a list, which is often generated using the `range()` function.

function A reusable bit of code. It can be reused without needing to rewrite the contents of the function. Instead, you call the function by using its name and any arguments it requires. It is possible to write your own functions.

game loop A type of `while` loop that is used to handle animations and user input in games. The reason that a loop is used is so that the program will repeatedly animate the screen and check for input instead of just doing it once.

graphical user interface (GUI) A program that uses graphics and icons for interaction with the users. GUIs use buttons, text boxes, sliders and a range of other things.

hexadecimal A numbering system that uses the numbers 0-9 and letters A-F for each digit. The letter A is the equivalent of the number 10, B = 11, C = 12, D = 13, E = 14 and F = 15.

hexadecimal colour code A colour system that uses hexadecimal numbers to represent colour values. Each primary colour—red, green and blue—is given a hexadecimal number between 00 and FF to state the intensity of that colour in the mix.

hit box Boxes used in video games when checking if a player, enemy, object or terrain are touching. They are usually rectangular in shape and surround the object representing the edges of where the game object will start to come into contact with other objects.

if statement Used in programs to decide whether or not to run a section of code. The decision is made based on a condition. Conditions are like questions, for example, "Is the price of the chocolate bar equal to the amount of money given for it?" or "Was the input equal to 'Yes'?". If the condition is True, then the code in the body of the if statement will run; otherwise, it will not.

integer A data type that is used to store whole numbers. For example, 1, 26 and 6546 are all whole numbers as they do not have a decimal place.

Integrated Development Environments (IDEs) Programs designed to help you develop your programs. They let you write, edit and save your programs just like a regular text editor, but also include other features for testing, debugging and running your programs.

keywords A set of reserved words that have a specific purpose in the programming language. As they are reserved, these words can't be used as the names of variables, functions or arguments. For example, the if keyword is used to create if statements so you can't use if as the name of a variable that you create.

module A set of pre-written functions that you can use with your programs. As modules are pre-written, they save you a lot of time as you don't have to write a lot of code yourself, most of which is often quite complex. Anyone can write modules and they enable your programs to do lots of things, from making games to manipulating images.

modulo operation (%) Similar to the division operator, but instead of evaluating to the value of one number divided by another, it evaluates to the value of the remainder of the division. For example, 7 % 3 is 1 as 7 / 3 is 2 remainder 1.

monospaced font A category of font where every letter, number and symbol is exactly the same width. Monospaced fonts are most often used to format code. They are also useful for displaying points and other information as you can predict the width of the text and get a consistent size.

named argument Used to explicitly state the values that you want to use for a function's argument. This is achieved by using the name of the argument in the function call.

nesting When one `if` statement or loop is located inside of another `if` statement or loop.

operating system The software that allows your computer to do its basic functions, such as allowing you to use mice and keyboards on the computer, save files and connect to the Internet. Microsoft Windows and Mac OS X are two examples of operating systems.

pixel A tiny dot on your computer monitor. Everything that is displayed on your monitor is made up of lots of pixels. The colour for each pixel is set by mixing the three primary colours: red, green and blue.

program A set of instructions that has been written by a programmer to instruct the computer to do something.

programming Using a set of instructions to tell a computer how to perform a task. These instructions are written in programming language.

programming language Allows you to give instructions to a computer. With a programming language you can create programs that control what your computer does. There are many different programming languages; Python, Java, Ruby and C++ are just a few of them.

property Data stored about a widget in `Tkinter`. For example, the text on a button is stored as a property, as is its size, colour and a whole load of other things.

Python shell A program that allows you to input one Python statement to be run at a time.

sprite A collection of images used to represent a character in games. Sprites include all of the images for the animations of a character that will be displayed in a game.

statement A single instruction of Python code. Statements are usually one line long, though some special statements can be several lines long. Statements are like a sentence in English and contain all the information Python needs to carry out a certain instruction, such as print a string or add two numbers together.

string A collection of characters—in other words, a piece of text. Strings are used to store letters, symbols and numbers together. They normally are surrounded by speech marks, such as `"Hello World"`.

syntax The set of rules about structure that a programming language must follow in order to work. Syntax is like the spelling and grammar in spoken and written language.

syntax errors These happen when you break the syntax rules of a programming language. If you don't follow the syntax rules, the computer will not understand what you are trying to do because it takes instructions literally and cannot guess what you mean if your syntax isn't quite right.

tremolo A sound effect where the volume of the sound increases and decreases in waves. As the music plays the volume of the music will increase and decrease, just as if you were turning the volume up and down really quickly. Tremolos can be used to make things sound spooky or exciting, depending on the speed.

tuple Like a list, a tuple holds a collection of items which can be stored in a single variable. Unlike a list, the values in a tuple cannot be changed after it has been created. When defining a tuple, all of the items in the tuple are enclosed in regular brackets () with commas to separate them.

type conversion When one data type is changed into another data type. For example, a string that contains a number could be changed into an integer, or an integer could be changed into a string.

variable Stores a value so that it can be reused later in a program. All variables have a name and a value. Variable names are used to identify the variable. The value of the variable can be a number, a string, a list of items and a few other things.

while loop Repeats a block of code. Like an `if` statement, it has a condition. The loop will only repeat if the condition is `True`. Every time the loop repeats, it will check if the condition is `True` or `False`. The loop will stop repeating if the condition changes to `False`.

widget A reusable GUI element in `Tkinter`. Buttons, sliders, text boxes and lots of other things are all widgets. They are used so that it is quick and easy to make programs.

x coordinate A number that measures your horizontal position (from left to right). The x coordinate starts at 0 at the left of the window and increases the farther right you move.

y coordinate A number that measures your vertical position (from top to bottom). The y coordinate starts at 0 at the top of the window and increases the farther down you go.

Index

SYMBOLS

+ (addition operator), 64
+= (addition operator, shorthand), 130
↵ character, 69
: (colon), use of, 40
>>> (command prompt), 17, 26, 251
/ (division operator), 64
/= (division operator, shorthand), 130
== (equal to) comparator, 40, 46, 67, 207
> (greater than) comparator, 67
>= (greater than or equal to) comparator, 67
(hash symbol) in hexadecimal colour code, 110
< (less than) comparator, 67
<= (less than or equal to) comparator, 67
% (modulo operator), 79, 207, 253
* (multiplication operator), 64
*= (multiplication operator, shorthand), 130
\n in string, 49
!= (not equal to) comparator, 46, 67
[] (square bracket), 98–99, 145
- (subtraction operator), 64
_ (underscore), 108

A

`aalines()` function, 177
`abs()` function, 214
Adafruit blog and learning site, 22
addition, using to draw spiral, 64–65
addition operator (+), 64
addition operator, shorthand (+=), 130
Adventures
    downloading files for, 248–250
    overview, 3, 4–5
Adventures in Python companion website, 20
Adventures in Raspberry Pi (Philbin), 241
Android operating system, 4
angle of line, changing, 61–63
animation
    game loop, 252
    teleportation, 197–201

two-player game, 234–236
walking
    adding sound and music, 218–219
    all directions, 195–197
    creating, 191–194
    wobbling circle, 133–135
anti-aliased line
    definition, 177, 251
    example of, 178
Apple operating system. *See* Mac OS X
argument
    `bg`, 112–113
    `column`, 116
    definition, 35, 251
    `from_`, 108
    `height`, 112–113
    named, 86, 87, 253
    naming, 108
    `row`, 116
    `width`, 112–113

B

background, transparent, 182–183, 185
`bg` argument, 112–113
black, hexadecimal colour code for, 111
blit, 183–184, 251
`blit()` function, 183, 186, 188
blog, Adafruit, 22
blue, hexadecimal colour code for, 111
book
    audience for, 3
    companion website, 20
    conventions, 20–21
    organisation of, 4–5
    screenshots for, 23
boolean, 126, 251
button
    `PyGame` module, creating in, 163–166
    `Tkinter` module
        changing text on click, 87–88
        counting clicks on, 88–89
        creating, 84–86

C

calling function, 74–75

canvas colour, changing, 111–113

`canvas` object, 111–113

capitalization in code, 29

cat image, 182–183

character control for two-player game, 234–236

`checkOffScreen()` function, 229, 231

`checkOffScreenX()` function, 149–150

`checkOffScreenY()` function, 149–150

circle

    drawing

        `PyGame` module, 124–127

        `turtle` module, 67–68

    wobbling, 133–135

`circle()` function, 125

CLI (command-line interface)

    definition, 84, 251

    keyboard and, 83

click speed game, creating, 117–119

code. *See also* function; statement; variable

    downloading from companion website, 33

    example of, 2

    indents in, 46

    repeating with loop, 45–48, 65–67

    reusing, 72–75

    spaces at start of line, 39

    speech (quotation) marks in, 18, 28

    syntax, 29, 254

    syntax error

        definition, 29, 255

        finding, 28–30

        x and y coordinates, 150

    typing and errors in, 37

Codecademy website, 21

coin collecting game, two-player, 234–237

collision

    code for, 152–154

    two-player game, 229–231, 237

colon (:), use of, 40

colour

    canvas colour, changing, 111–113

    of exploding clicks, 169–171

    filling in shape with, 71–72

    as hexadecimal value, 109–111, 253

colour grid, creating, 131–132

colour picker

    creating, 113–116

    slider, creating, 105–109

    text box, adding, 116–117

`colour` variable, 112–113, 115, 130

`column` argument, 116

command prompt (>>>)

    definition, 17, 251

    IDLE program, 26

command quick reference table

    Adventure 1, 55

    Adventure 2, 79–80

    Adventure 4, 120

    Adventure 5, 137

    Adventure 6, 159

    Adventure 7, 178

    Adventure 8, 201

    Adventure 9, 220

command-line interface (CLI)

    definition, 84, 251

    keyboard and, 83

comparator

    definition, 67, 251

    equals (==), 40, 46, 67, 207

    greater than (>), 67

    greater than or equal to (>=), 67

    less than (<), 66

    less than or equal to (<=), 67

    not equal to (!=), 46, 67

computer, programming, 24

concatenation

    definition, 35, 251

    example, 34

conditional

    `elif` statement, 44, 252

    `else` statement, 40, 44, 252

    `if` statement, 39–41, 67, 164, 253

    nested `if` statement, 41–43

    vending machine, creating imaginary, 43–45

console for spaceship control

    overview, 50

    set-up and password, 50–52

    uses for, 52–54

conventions, 20–21

coordinate

    definition, 146, 251

    mouse input, 161

    moving player around screen, 145–146

    x coordinate, 146, 255

    y coordinate, 146, 255

`cos()` function, 134

`count` variable, 89, 171

counting, hexadecimal, 110